Embroidered Alphabets

With Ribbon Embroidery

Embroidered
DI VAN NIEKERK Alphabets

With Ribbon Embroidery

Search Press

This book is dedicated to Werner Etsebeth – thank you for your patience and panache.

Acknowledgements:
Thank you to Debra Jordan Bryan and Steve Bryan for the two Angel designs on page 128. These beautiful images are sure to captivate embroiderers and quilters worldwide. I love your artwork Debra! Thank you to Verde for helping to paint the water-colours. As always, it is a pleasure to work with you. To my friends Emma Kriegler and Carol Carl, thank you for helping with the embroidery. What would I do without you? And to all embroiderers worldwide, thank you for your encouragement and support.

First published in Great Britain 2009
Search Press Limited
Wellwood, North Farm Road, Tunbridge Wells, Kent TN2 3DR

Originally published in South Africa in 2009 under the title *Monograms and words in ribbon embroidery* by Metz Press
1 Cameronians Ave, Welgemoed, South Africa

ISBN: 978-1-84448-446-1

Publisher	Wilsia Metz
Design and lay-out	Liezl Maree
Illustrations	Wendy Brittnell
Photographer	Ivan Naudé
Reproduction	Color/Fuzion
Printed and bound in Singapore	
	by Tien Wah Press

Contents

Introduction

George Eliot wrote: *What do we live for, if it is not to make life less difficult for each other?* This book would like to do just that – make life less difficult by inspiring you to create something more special than anything you could have bought for a friend or member of your family. Time and again, I mull over what I should make for a special friend or family member to show thanks, or to celebrate a special occasion. I am sure you do too! We have all learnt the value of family and friends, have come to realise how fortunate we are to have them in our lives. Now you can show how them how precious they are to you, by making them something unique.

Babies are our most treasured gift; shopping for just the right present for a special infant can be a daunting task, what with the myriad of products to choose from. Where do you find a gift that is extraordinary and does not appear to be mass-produced? Now you have the solution …

This book will teach you how to embroider a baby's name and how to use it on a teddy bear which may just become a treasured heirloom for the child to take to university or college one day. It will show you how to apply names, words and sentences onto other items such as blankets, toys, handbags, beanies, bibs for little tots. You will have lots of fun as the possibilities are endless. Imagine how rewarding it is to give a personalised present for a 16th or 21st birthday, a housewarming or a 10th wedding anniversary. No matter what the occasion, using the ideas in this book you can be confident that your gift is really one of a kind –

you will have the freedom to create delightful projects in no time at all.

You will learn how to personalise gifts for weddings – monogrammed pillowcases or linen, a valentine's gift for that special person in your life; gifts for birthdays, graduations, Christmas; lovely place mats for a new home, a personalised wooden box which contains a gift for a kitchen tea or stork party to be used afterwards for towels and soaps in a guest bathroom; make a name tag for your daughter's bedroom door or decorate her wall with the word *Love*.

Learn how to make your own cards and gift tags; thank-you gifts are always welcome too. Included are different ideas for showing people courtesy and kindness. Perhaps your neighbour or a colleague is going through a rough patch – make a small personalised gift to cheer her up; let her know that you are thinking of her. To quote W G Paulson Townsend: *Embroidery is a very personal art; its charm lies in the individuality expressed by the worker.*

This book will certainly enable you to convey your unique message whenever you need a special gift, an unusual fashion accessory, or a piece to decorate a home.

Above all, enjoy yourself. I do hope that your creations will bring you, your friends and your family much enchantment and joy.

Di van Niekerk

HOW TO USE THIS BOOK

This book has been written in such a way that it will enable even the beginner to ribbon embroidery to prepare and embroider beautiful monograms, names and words. Stitches are shown in the stitch gallery on pages 52 to 58, and soon you will be familiar with the flowers, leaves and shapes used to embellish the monogram, initial and words. Every letter of the alphabet is shown step-by step on pages 60 to 111, with a list of what you need for each letter; you will be surprised at how little you actually need to make a beautiful gift.

The designs at the back of the book are ideal for cards and wall plaques. Or use them in a quilt, to cover a journal, for a lid on a trinket or memory box, on a recipe folder or a tote bag. Change the words to suit the occasion – make a ring cushion using the design of the *I love you* card, for instance. Make a framed picture for a precious mom based on the *Happy Birthday* or *Thank you* cards. Find the correct translations

for the words and messages and embroider them for friends in their own language. But I am getting ahead of myself – more about changing words and sentences into other languages on page 14.

The borders on pages 116 and 125 are ideal for sewing on either side of a monogram for a pillowcase, sheet or towel; or use a border along the sides of a box, to decorate a handbag, along the hem of a monogrammed T-shirt or jeans. You will probably have many creative ideas no one else has thought of before.

Depending on how much work you want to put into the design, on who will be receiving your gift, depending on the occasion, you have choices when making the monograms or words in this book. For instance, I used the D on page 66 to make the lid of a memory box for my mom to remember my late twin brother on his 50th birthday. I wanted to make a special gift for this occasion and embroidered as much detail on the D as possible. However, if you are making a wedding present for a casual acquaintance, you may not want to spend hours embroidering the

monogram. Then use the painted detail to do most of the work for you and only embroider the stems, roses and leaves, as I did with the Dream journal on page 10. The completed journal is beautiful, although the letter D is not filled in with stitches.

The letters have been painted in watercolour and you will find these on pages 121 to 125 for scanning and/or copying and printing. Throughout the book you will find pictures to inspire and guide you with good ideas, as well as handy hints and tips. There are lovely templates at the back of the book for quicker projects, which you will be able to copy yourself with a scanner and printer. If you are good with computers, there are some excellent programs you can use to design your own monograms, words, names, and sentences. If you are not keen on using a computer, you could ask us (or a friend) to help you create your design. There are various image-editing programs for quilters and embroiderers wishing to use words and letters in their projects. You can create gorgeous designs incorporating the watercolour monograms and pictures in the back of this book using some of the simpler programs; more about this on page 13.

For your convenience, you could also use our personalised service and order your artwork (monograms, words, cards, sentences or names directly from us). Let us have the details you wish to embroider and we will create and email you a unique design. Download the image onto a portable storage device, such as a memory stick or a CD, and ask your nearest copy shop to print it onto fabric of your own choice. We can also print your design onto our PFP (prepared for printing) heirloom cotton and post the printed panel on to you, wherever you are in the world. Visit our website www.dicraft.co.za or e-mail me at di@dicraft.co.za for advice about designing your artwork.

Monograms, letters and words

In this book you will be using monograms, initials and letters to create most of your embroidered artwork. Before we start, the following information will guide you:

A **monogram** is a specially designed decorative image of a single initial, or a combination of two or more letters that are grouped or intertwined. Monograms are often embroidered on linen, clothing and so on, or printed on stationery.

An **initial** is a letter at the beginning of a word. It is sometimes lavishly adorned and often much larger than the rest of the text, used in printing and embroidery.

A **letter** is a character or a symbol that is part of an alphabet used in printing or writing.

HOW ARE MONOGRAMS USED?

There are several choices when creating a monogram – use a single initial, or two, three or four, depending on the occasion, the situation and the gift.

Personal monogram

Often a monogram is designed with the initials of our names. The monogram can be styled in a number of ways by using one or more initials.

SINGLE LETTER

When one large single letter is used, it is the first initial of the person's first or last name. **Diana Ella Handley's** single-letter monogram will be

TWO-LETTER MONOGRAM

Two letters representing the person's first and last names. **Diana Ella Handley's** two-letter monogram will be

THREE-LETTER MONOGRAM

For a three-letter monogram there are two options. If you make all the letters the same size, the monogram is in the order you would write the name: the first initial, followed by the middle and last initials.

Using different sizes, you place the initial of the last name in the centre and make it larger than the initials of the first and second names flanking it.

A monogram for a couple

Today, a three-letter monogram is the most fashionable for couples, although a single or two-letter monogram is also a popular choice.

SINGLE LETTER

When one large letter is used as a monogram for a couple, as a rule it is the first initial of the couple's last name. **Diana and Gary Hobson's** monogram would be

TWO-LETTER MONOGRAM

Two letters represent the initials of the couple's first names. **Diana and Gary Hobson's** two-letter monogram would be

THREE-LETTER MONOGRAM

Monograms are always read from left to right. The bride's first-name initial is typically placed first in a monogram, followed by their last name initial (usually larger) and the groom's first-name initial. **Diana and Gary Hobson's** monogram will be

Some folks prefer the groom's initial to be placed first (on the left) followed by the bride's initial last (on the right); both are acceptable. If you know the bride well, her initial could be first; if the groom is a friend or family member, his initial could be placed first. To monogram a feminine gift, such as linen or a journal, it is a good idea to place the bride's initial first. If the gift is more masculine, place the groom's initial first. If you know Gary well and the gift is masculine, the monogram could be

FOUR-LETTER MONOGRAM

If the gift is for a couple where the bride has kept her last name, a four-letter monogram is suitable. The layout would be the bride's first name, the bride's last name, the groom's last name and the groom's first

name. Therefore **Diana Handley-Hobson and Gary Hobson's** monogram would be

or

DESIGN IDEAS FOR MONOGRAMS

There are so many possibilities for monograms. These ideas will help you to create a monogram for your specific project. Read more about creating your design on pages 15 to 16, and about printing your design on pages 16 to 20.

If you are good with computers, there are some excellent image-editing programs that enable you to design your own monograms, words, names, and sentences.

Monograms without borders

SINGLE ORNATE MONOGRAMS

Designs for all the letters of the alphabet are printed in full colour on pages 121 to 125. Copy these onto your chosen fabric or have this done at a copy shop. Step by step instructions to embroider them are on pages 60 to 111.

A single ornate monogram is useful for personalising linen, a lid of a trinket box, a journal, a dress pocket, a little tote bag and countless other projects that you can think of. Use the initial of the person's name or surname as the embroidery for a unique gift.

MONOGRAMS WITH MORE THAN ONE LETTER

Place the ornate initial in the centre and add plain letters alongside in pencil or a water-soluble pen. Embroider the ornate initial as shown on pages 60 to 111; embroider the black and white initials alongside in whipped back-stitch or whipped chain-stitch (see pages 47 and 48).

A monogram with more than one letter is ideal for a wedding gift, to decorate the lid of a memory box, a beautiful pillow or to cover a journal that a couple can use for wedding pictures.

Monograms with borders

A monogram surrounded by a border makes a beautiful personalised gift for a wedding couple, a best friend, or family member.

CREATING AN ORNATE INITIAL SURROUNDED BY A BORDER

You will find the borders on pages 116 to 118; choose any initial from pages 121 to 125. There are a number of choices for getting the design onto fabric when creating this kind of monogram.

- Scan the border and initial in colour, place the initial in the border using an image-editing program and print onto fabric. See pages 15 to 21.
- Scan, enlarge and print the border onto fabric. Trace the initial in the border, using a sharp pencil or water-soluble pen.

- Trace both the border and initial onto fabric, using a sharp pencil or water-soluble pen.

Embroider the design following the instructions for the border on pages 116 to 118 and for the initial on pages 60 to 111.

I have included borders for monograms on pages 125 and 126. Here are some ideas for this kind of monogram:

ROUND BORDER WITH N

Scan the border and initial in colour, place the initial in the border using an image-editing program and print onto fabric. Or trace both border and initial, using a sharp pencil or water-soluble pen. Embroider the border and initial in colour (see instructions for the border on page 117 and for the initial on pages 86 to 87).

HORSESHOE BORDER

Scan the border and initial in colour, place the initials in the border using an image-editing program and print onto fabric. Or trace both border and initial with a pencil or water-soluble pen. Embroider the border and initial in colour (see instructions for the border on page 118). The initials are embroidered in whipped back or chain stitch (see pages 47 and 48).

MONOGRAMS BETWEEN STRAIGHT BORDERS

Embroider borders on both sides of a monogram when working along the hem of a pillowcase, a sheet or table napkin. I have included straight borders on page 125 with instructions on page 116.

DESIGN IDEAS USING WORDS, NAMES AND SENTENCES

The power of **words** cannot be underestimated – words to comfort a sick grandmother, words to encourage a new mom or a newly married friend, inspiring words that express your feelings, words that motivate and give confidence. Words can be prepared and embroidered onto fabric. Attach this to a T-shirt, a toy, a lovely piece of linen, a handmade card, handbag, box, or journal; whatever you think will be an appropriate gift for the recipient. Express your thoughts and feelings in an embroidered piece that is one of a kind.

A round monogram – a perfect circle with words such as *love, faith, cherish, forever* – is ideal for a wedding or engagement present.

For the first ornate letter of the word, use one of the painted initials on pages 121 to 125; scan the initial. Use image-editing software and work in layers to create the rest of the word. Print and transfer as explained on pages 16 to 21. Alternatively, trace the initial with pencil or water-soluble pen. For instructions on embroidering the letters, see pages 60 to 111.

Place mats   Soft toy

Names are precious too. A baby's name embroidered and sewn onto a blanket or teddy bear turns the item into a treasured heirloom. Embroider the name of a good friend or sibling and cover a journal, or attach it to the centre of a cushion or handbag. Use one of the painted initials in this book on pages 121 to 125 to form the first letter of the name and add the remaining letters of the name. For instructions on embroidering the letters, see pages 47 and 48.

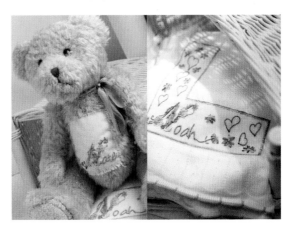

Teddy   Blanket

Phrases consist of words that are grouped together, for example *Welcome Home Princess, Friends Forever, I love you, Happy Birthday, Congratulations, Thank you my friend, With love, You are an Angel,* and, embroidered, can turn various items into great gifts for a special event. Use one of the painted initials in this book on pages 121 to 125 to form the first letter

of the sentence and add the text that follows (see page 16). For instructions on embroidering the letters, see pages 60 to 111, and 47 to 48.

Embroider a meaningful note to a special friend using a short sentence or phrase such as *Live, laugh, love and good luck my friend*. Trace a pattern onto fabric in pencil or water-soluble pen and embellish it with a bit of embroidery. Cut out and glue onto a trinket box or card.

Phrases like *Good friends, good food, good times* can be printed onto placemats and used as a wedding gift. They need not be embroidered at all (see image on page 13); for quicker projects you do not always have to embroider the image.

The *You are an angel* design on page 8 is ideal for tags for scrapbooking, or use as a gift tag. Scan and print it onto fabric (see page 16). To make a pretty framed picture as a thank-you gift for a special person, embroider the roses and leaves with ribbon as shown on page 112. Fill in the remaining letters of the word in whipped back or chain stitch as shown on page 47.

The other tag designs on page 8 are handy for printing onto fabric to embroider. The tags add a unique touch to a special gift and the recipient can frame them; your work will be remembered for a very long time and become a treasured keepsake. For a quick project, only embroider the flowers of the ornate letter and

- if the remaining letters of the words are tiny, use one or two strands of thread instead of ribbon

and work them in whipped back or chain stitch as shown on pages 47 and 48.
- leave the remaining letters as they are – it is not essential to embroider the letters.

On pages 127 and 128 you will find lovely designs for cards or for embroidery and framing. Embroider a unique project that is both a card and a gift (see pages 15 to 21 for instructions on transferring the design). For the instructions on embroidering these designs, see pages 112 to 115, and 119 to 120.

WORDS IN DIFFERENT LANGUAGES

Words such as *Dream, Joy, Love, Memories, Angel, Cherish, Welcome, Thank you*, all convey a special meaning to the receiver of your gift. These words can be translated into different languages to suit the recipient. It is such fun to be able to embroider in other languages. Type in the word *translate* using an Internet search engine and you will find different websites that translate words for you. If possible, find a mother-tongue speaker of the language to check the translations, though, as the Internet programs do not translate in context and are flawed. They seem unable to distinguish between verbs and nouns, among others.

The Russian publisher of *A perfect world in ribbon embroidery and stumpwork* was kind enough to send me the Russian translation of several words I then embroidered and used on special gift items.

If you wish to translate a word into a language that uses the Arabic, Cyrillic, Hebrew or Greek alphabets, for instance, find a copy of the relevant alphabet (widely available on the Internet) and see if any of the painted letters from our alphabet on pages 121 to 125 can be reversed or used in any other way to form the initial of the word. Then use a font in the alphabet you require to make up the rest of the word. I reversed the E on to form the word *Cherish* in Russian for a scarf (see page 50). You can also glue the word onto a pretty box for gift for a kitchen tea. To embroider the Russian word for *baby*, I scanned an M initial on the computer and the remaining letters were printed in a font that uses the Cyrillic alphabet. The embroidered word was then sewn onto a mischievous little soft toy sheep (see photograph on page 7).

For this handbag I used the Russian word meaning love. *You can also use it on a baby's bib or on a hot-water bottle.*

So, don't be deterred by words in other languages; find a word that uses one of the painted letters in the book for the first initial, reverse the letter if necessary. Print out the rest of the word in the relevant script. Embroider the ornate initial as shown on pages 121 to 125 and the rest of the word in whipped back or chain stitch (see pages 47 and 48).

Creating and transferring designs

There are several ways to create a design and print and transfer it onto fabric for embroidery. The easiest way is to choose your monograms and borders, decide how you want to combine them and have it done at a copy shop, or to order it from us or one of our stockists and get on with the embroidery right away.

USE THE PICTURES IN THE BOOK

On pages 127 and 128 you will find pictures to copy, print and transfer onto fabric. You could also order the printed pictures on cloth directly from our distributors or from our website. Make a lovely card for a special friend or family member and embroider it to be framed as a keepsake. Follow the instructions on pages 112 to 115, and 119 to 120 for the embroidery.

The tags on page 8 are ideal to print onto fabric and embroider the ornate initials, flowers and leaves. Leave the remaining letters as they are, or embroider them with one or two strands of silk or cotton thread in whipped back or chain stitch (see pages 47 and 48).

The borders on page 125 are perfect for stitching on either side of a monogram or word. They are designed to be repeated to fit the size of the project you are embroidering.

DO YOUR OWN SCANNING/COPYING AND PRINTING

If you know your way around scanners, computers and printers, you will have great fun scanning in the monograms and templates and creating your own unique designs using image editing programs. These designs can then be printed straight onto fabric, ensuring that you follow all manufacturer's instructions throughout the process, or onto heat transfer paper and ironed onto fabric, again following all manufacturer's instructions.

I have compiled detailed information on the scanning, printing and image editing process, but this became rather lengthy and technical and had to be sacrificed to make way for more templates in the book. You will find the detailed information on our website at www.dicraft.co.za, so go there if you want to learn more about using scanners, printers and image editing programs for embroidery projects.

Using heat-transfer paper

Heat-transfer paper is a heavy paper that absorbs the ink from the printer. You then use heat and a considerable amount of pressure to transfer the ink onto the fabric. The paper backing is peeled off, either while it is still hot (hot peel), or once it's cold (cold peel). Hot-peel transfers are softer and more pliable, whereas the cold-peel transfers sometimes allow for heavy ink deposits and have a rubbery texture. The softer the print, the easier it is to embroider; try several brands to find the texture you are happy with.

Inkjet heat-transfer paper, also known as iron-on transfer paper or T-shirt transfer paper, is available from stationery, quilting, art and craft, and T-shirt or copy shops. Images on this paper are easier to iron onto fabric. The inkjet printer does not expose the paper to heat, therefore the printed design requires less heat to transfer onto fabric. You can use a normal iron to transfer the image onto fabric – read the manufacturer's instructions before you start (see Which fabric to use on page 21).

A **laser heat-transfer** is exposed to heat when it is printed and will therefore require a much hotter temperature to transfer it onto fabric. This is why a heat press is normally required for large laser transfers. But you can do smaller transfers that will fit under the plate of an iron (see Ironing hot-peel transfers at home on page 17).

We use colour-laser copiers, as do most of the copy shops, using specific transfer paper for specific

---

HINTS

- The **easiest** printer to use is the **inkjet** printer as the transfer paper for this printer allows you to iron the transfer onto fabric with an ordinary iron. It can also print onto pre-treated fabric sheets.
- Before buying inkjet transfer-paper or pre-treated fabric sheets, ensure that your inkjet printer can print onto heavier paper stock or iron-on transfer paper.
- If you are using heat transfer-sheets or the solvent method (see page 20), reverse the image (flip horizontally) so that it is a mirror image of the original. If you are printing directly onto a pre-treated fabric sheet, do not reverse the image.
- Always test a transfer on a similar piece of scrap fabric before you start.

machines. If you are using our personalised service, or that of a copy shop, don't be too concerned about the technical details; the copy shop attendant will print your design onto transfer paper for you. If they do not have the fabric suitable for ribbon embroidery, take your fabric to the copy shop; they will print the transfer onto the fabric with a commercial heat press. If they do not have a heat press, take the transfer to a T-shirt printing shop that uses a heat press, or, if it is small enough, iron it on at home (see Ironing hot-peel transfers at home opposite).

Inkjet paper **cannot** be used in a laser printer or copier as it will melt with the heat that is generated in the transfer process. The same applies when printing directly onto fabric using pre-treated fabric sheets (see page 18).

PRINTING THE HEAT TRANSFER

Always print a preview copy of your artwork onto normal photocopy paper to check that the image is positioned correctly, that you are happy with the colours, whether the image has been reversed and to check on the size before printing it onto costly transfer paper. What you see on your screen may not necessarily be what is printed on the paper. Adjust if necessary and only then print the image onto the transfer sheet.

Insert one sheet into the printer at a time, ensuring that you have the right side up or down, depending on your printer. Read the manufacturer's instructions carefully to determine the right and wrong side. The paper is usually marked on the wrong side. You may be able to fit two images onto one transfer sheet to save on costs. Use normal to low print quality – you should not over-saturate the transfer with ink as the fabric may not be able to absorb all the ink and the image may bleed and become blurred. Try to use the heat transfer on the day it was printed – fresh transfers do give a better image. Remember to allow inkjet paper to dry before transferring the image onto fabric.

IRONING HOT-PEEL TRANSFERS AT HOME

Always read the manufacturer's instructions on the heat-transfer pack before you start.

Don't use an ironing board as it is too soft and does not retain enough heat. Prepare a firm, smooth, padded board that is larger than the transfer sheet. If the transfer overlaps the board, its edge will form an unsightly mark. Set the board on a work table and cover it with a cotton pillowcase or old sheet. The cover must be absolutely smooth – check that there are no wrinkles, and that it is the same thickness throughout.

A heat transfer requires a high temperature for a good finish. The best iron to use is the older type with no steam vents. If you use a steam iron, set it off-steam to the highest temperature that the background fabric will allow.

Iron the padded surface until it is very hot. This ensures a better transfer. Centre the prepared fabric (see page 22) right side up on the heated surface. Iron the fabric to remove any moisture. Wait for it to cool slightly and place the prepared transfer sheet right side down in the centre of the fabric.

1. Place the hot iron in the centre of the transfer, moving it very slowly and applying as much pressure with the iron as possible. Press down hard for 20 to 30 seconds per section. Apply the heat as evenly

as possible, before moving on. Start in the centre and work in a circular movement towards the outer edges to prevent air bubbles from forming.

2. Keep your arms straight and press down as hard as you can.

3. Iron the transfer again so that the entire sheet is heated once more. The paper should be hot in all areas before you peel it off. While the transfer is still hot, lift a corner to see if all or most of the colour is on your fabric. If not, iron the transfer again, using more pressure and heat. If the image looks good, start peeling the transfer while it is still hot.

4. Hold the fabric down on the board and peel off the backing with one continuous movement; work with a fast and even tension from side to side or top to bottom. **Caution: remember that the heat transfer will be hot.** Avoid peeling from corner to corner (on the bias) as this may distort the fabric. If the paper doesn't peel easily, because it has cooled down, re-heat this section again and peel as you heat.

5. Gently stretch the fabric by pulling along the edges while it is still flat on the ironing surface. This will even out any distortions caused by the peeling. Don't wash the transfer for 24 to 48 hours – it is not really necessary to wash it anyway, as you would have prepared your fabric beforehand (see Preparing the fabric on page 22).

INKJET PRINTING ONTO PRE-TREATED FABRIC-SHEETS

Pre-treated printable sheets of fabric, bonded to paper to stabilise the fabric so that it won't jam in your printer, are available from stationery, art and craft and quilting shops or websites. These sheets are often pre-treated with a fixative rendering the inks colour-fast; they are washable and fade-resistant. Try to use only the pre-treated sheets. If the fabric sheets are creased, iron them before you print; the fabric must be as smooth as possible for a good print. Do not use a steam iron; steam may form watermarks and cause the backing to split from the fabric.

Once the fabric is printed and the inks have dried, the paper backing is removed. Follow the manufacturer's instructions for printing and treating the fabric after printing. Set your printer to A4 or letter size, depending on your pack, using a thick paper setting, if possible.

Do **not** reverse your image for this method and place the fabric side up or down depending on your printer's feed mechanism. If your printer turns the paper as it feeds, place the sheet in the tray with the fabric side down. Only feed one sheet at a time after removing all normal paper from the tray. Depending on the manufacturer, once the ink has dried, you may have to iron the fabric (don't use steam) to heat-set the ink.

MAKING YOUR OWN PRINTABLE FABRIC SHEETS

This method is not suitable for babies' toys, clothing or any item that a baby may chew.

Pre-treat fabric with an ink fixative such as *Bubble Jet Set 2000* or *Amafu Ink-Jet-Set* for use with inkjet printers to render the printed fabric colourfast and washable. *Bubble Jet Set 2000* is available online or from quilting shops worldwide and *Amafu Ink-Jet-Set* is available in South Africa. Follow the manufacturer's instructions on the ink fixative bottle; use rubber gloves and work in a well-ventilated area. Soak the fabric in the solution and hang up to dry.

Now you need to fix the fabric onto a temporary backing so that you will be able to feed it through your inkjet printer. The temporary backing should not leave any residue on the fabric once it is removed; therefore you may want to experiment with different products to find the backing that suits you best

A popular backing for printable fabric is **freezer paper** – a plastic-coated white paper used for wrapping food before freezing. *Reynolds® Freezer Paper* is sold in the USA and is available to other countries from quilting websites and stores. Re-usable, pre-cut freezer-paper sheets, cut to fit in your printer, are also available online and from quilting or arts and craft shops. Prepare an ironing surface as for ironing a transfer (see page 17).

Cut a sheet of pre-treated fabric about 1 cm (^{3}/$_8$ in.) larger than A4 printer paper all round. Cut the freezer paper A4 size – as it will be smaller than the fabric there won't be any residue flaking onto the ironing surface (or iron) as you press it onto the fabric. Set the iron on a cotton setting (no steam) if you use cotton; for silk, use a medium setting. Place the fabric, wrong side up on the ironing surface with the freezer paper shiny side down on the wrong side of the fabric. Iron the paper onto the fabric, smoothing out any creases as you iron from the centre outwards. Once the paper is fused to the fabric, especially along the edges, turn fabric side up and iron gently to remove any wrinkles. Use a cotton or Teflon pressing-cloth to avoid marking your fabric. Neatly trim the fabric and backing to about 2 mm (^{1}/$_{16}$ in.) smaller to prevent it from jamming your printer. Remove any bits of thread or fluff on the fabric so they won't spoil the printed image or get caught up in your printer.

Peel-off A4 adhesive labels (one label on a page) available from stationery or office supply websites and stores can also be used as backing. The label is peeled off the backing and pressed down onto the wrong side of the fabric. Be sure to remove all the air bubbles for a good print. Use a small, clean baking or wallpaper roller or cold iron to remove any air bubbles and trim.

Repositionable **spray adhesives**, such as *Sulky KK2000* or *Madeira MSA 1100*, are commonly used for appliqué and quilting. These spray adhesives are absorbed into the fibres of the fabric and disappear within two to five days. Spray the glue onto a sheet of printer paper (follow the manufacturer's instructions – don't hold the can too close to the paper), place the treated fabric wrong side down onto the glued paper. Use a small baking or wallpaper roller or cold iron to remove all the air bubbles for a smooth print, and trim.

It is advisable to use the prepared fabric sheets soon after they have been treated and stabilised with a backing; fresh sheets do print better. Use as you would pre-treated fabric sheets.

- Make sure that the short edge that is fed into the printer first, is firmly attached to the backing to avoid jamming your printer. If necessary, use a piece of masking tape along this edge.
- If the 'sandwich' curls up as it prints, use a ruler to gently hold it down while it feeds into the printer.
- Carefully remove the print to avoid smudging the inks.
- Once the inks have dried, remove the backing, wash the fabric with a gentle liquid detergent or use *Bubble Jet Rinse* (follow the manufacturer's directions). Rinsing the fabric removes the excess ink which prevents bleeding.

TRANSFERRING IMAGES USING THE SOLVENT METHOD

The solvent process is used to lift the toner off the paper onto your fabric. The result is a faded, worn look that could be just what you need for your project. This method can only be used with mirror-image laser prints from laser copiers and printers.

Solvents such as lacquer thinners, turpentine, and acetone are generally used. Some crafters have successfully used *Citra-Solve* or wintergreen oil, available from health shops. For smaller transfers you could try a clear blender pen available from art and craft shops. These pens are dual-tipped markers filled with a solvent such as xylene – highly toxic, but safe if you follow the safety precautions.

Your image must be printed on glossy paper which allows the toner to sit on top of the paper, ensuring a better transfer. If the print does not transfer onto fabric, try different papers. Some papers absorb the toner; some are too coated for the solvent to penetrate the paper. Experiment until you find paper and solvent that work.

Place your background fabric right side up on a hard, clean, flat board. Secure the fabric in place with masking tape so that it will not move or wrinkle in the next step. Lay the printed paper right side down on the fabric. Use masking tape to secure the print onto the fabric at the two top corners. Carefully pour the solvent onto a square of cotton gauze or a small ball of cotton wool. (Replace the bottle top so the solvent won't tip out.) Dab the wrong side of the print with the solvent; don't get it too wet, but apply enough to make the paper look semi-transparent. Rub over the damp paper with the back of a spoon, applying pressure to move the toner onto the fabric. Work from the centre outwards in circular movements; ensure that you rub the entire image to prevent blank spots. Lift one corner gently to check on the image, taking care not to move the paper as this will cause the image to blur. If the image is very faded, add more solvent and use more pressure on the spoon. Work quickly before the solvent dries. If necessary, apply more solvent and rub again until the transfer is successful.

Once the image is transferred, allow the fabric to dry overnight; iron the back of the cloth to heat set. Gently wash the printed fabric in a bucket of soapy, tepid water, rinse well. Hang up to dry and iron whilst still damp to remove the creases before you begin to embroider.

CAUTION

- This method is not recommended for babies' toys, clothing (or any item that a baby may chew on) **unless** you have carefully and thoroughly rinsed out all the solvent after transfer and before embroidering your design.
- Do not use this method when you're pregnant as the solvents may harm the unborn foetus.
- Work outdoors or in a well-ventilated area and use rubber gloves.
- Keep children and pets away from your work area.
- Do not smoke or work near an open flame – most of these solvents are flammable.
- Keep the tools (such as spoons) away from the kitchen; wash and store them separately.
- Wash hands well after use.

Which fabric to use

Pure cotton is the best fabric to use for inkjet and laser transfer-paper, as well as laser copies for the solvent method. For ribbon embroidery, a soft and smooth, medium-weight cotton with a high thread count is ideal. It should have a dull, matt finish – no shine – and wash well. The fabric must be strong enough to hold all the stitches in the design without puckering out of shape; the weave must not be so tight that it will be difficult to pull the ribbon through, nor so loose that the cotton is unable to support the stitches. Although a looser-weave fabric is easier to work on, you will soon become used to using a thicker cenille needle which makes a large enough hole in the fabric for the ribbon to pass through easily. The finest quality cotton is Egyptian or combed cotton.

Inkjet heat transfers can be printed on most natural fabrics and some on 50/50 cotton/polycotton blends as well. Polycotton blends should be of medium weight so the fabric will not pull out of shape when you peel off the backing paper. Read the instructions on the transfer-paper pack before purchasing your fabric. Experiment with different cottons, linens and polycottons to find one that accepts the transfer and the heat. Polycotton blends tend to make the transfer more plastic; if your transfer paper does this, rather use pure cotton as a background fabric.

Smooth cotton allows for a clear transfer. Natural fabrics like Dupion silk and linens woven from irregular, slightly twisted, uneven yarns are not always smooth enough for heat transfers, but if you like an uneven effect, experiment until you find the texture that you like.

For printing directly onto fabric, use a good quality pure cotton fabric with a high thread count and a smooth texture. Prepare the fabric as described on page 19.

Apart from the design for the bag on page 15, which was done on pale, hand-dyed linen, all the designs were printed on white or off-white cotton. The light colour ensures a good, crisp image. Remember, the fabric on which you are printing becomes the background of your design. Transfer paper is semi-translucent; too dark a background and you won't be able to see the outlines. To prevent the monogram, word or picture from being too dark to embroider, choose lighter shades of fabric – white or off-white is best.

If you plan to use a dark colour for your project, a red blanket or a green beanie, for example, it is a good idea to transfer your artwork onto white fabric, embroider it, cut out the embroidered block or strip and attach it to the dark fabric (see Attaching the embroidery to the project, pages 49 to 51).

If you choose to trace your design with a pencil, water-soluble pen, or a *Pigma Micron*® pen you have more freedom in the choice of your fabric. Linen, cotton, polycotton or silk are all good choices. The only requirements in this case are that the fabric complements the design, is easy to work on, that the traced lines will be visible and that the fabric is strong enough to hold all the stitches.

PREPARING THE FABRIC

Some cotton fabrics have invisible finishes that interfere with the toners, inks, or chemicals used to transfer designs or that may scorch in the transfer process. The fabric should be washed to remove sizing and finishes such as starch, glaze and oil, so that the ink or toner remains on the fabric when it is washed.

In general, the cheaper the cloth, the more sizing it contains. To prepare your fabric for printing, wash it at the highest temperature the fabric will allow. Use ordinary liquid detergent or washing powder and don't wring the fabric; hang it up to dry and press with a steam iron whilst still damp. The fabric must be free of creases before you print or transfer any images.

Sometimes, nothing you do can remove all the finishes. Experiment with different fabrics to find one that takes the transfer well. Ask your supplier for PFP (prepared for printing) fabric; if you have difficulty obtaining this, you are welcome to contact us to supply you.

Remember that you need to stretch your design in a hoop for embroidery, so cut your fabric at least 7,5 cm (3 in.) larger than the span of the hoop. This way, you will easily fit and stretch the fabric in the hoop before tightening the screw. For example, for a 20 cm (8 in.) hoop, your fabric should be about 27,5 cm (11 in.) square. The embroidered design is cut to size once you have completed it.

Before you start

GETTING THE SIZE RIGHT

When enlarging or reducing the size of the design to suit your specific project, use wider or narrower ribbon to compensate for the change in size. For example, for a smaller design, use a narrower ribbon to suit the smaller flowers and leaves: rather than 7 mm ribbon, use 4 mm ribbon; instead of 4 mm use 2 mm ribbon. The same applies to threads – the thicker perlé thread may be too bulky for a smaller design; rather use one or two strands of cotton, rayon, or silk. The opposite applies to enlarged designs.

To enlarge (or reduce) an initial or design use the following formula: required size divided by given size multiplied by 100. Say you want an initial to be 10 cm (4 in.) high and in this book it is 5 cm (2 in.) high. Using the formula: 10 ÷ 5 x 100 = 200 gives you the percentage at which you need to print it on the copier. The width will automatically be enlarged by 200% to accommodate the height.

Use the same formula to reduce the size that you want: required size divided by given size multiplied by 100. Say you want a picture to be 5 cm (4 in.) high and in this book it is 7,5 cm (3 in.) high. Using the formula: 5 ÷ 7,5 x 100 = 66 gives you the percentage at which you need to print it on the copier. If the formula sounds too complicated, don't be deterred; the technician at the copy shop should know all about it!

BACKING FABRIC

For flimsier embroidery backgrounds it is a good idea to add an extra layer of fabric at the back of the printed block to stabilise it. Choose a soft polysilk, cotton muslin or a fine polycotton and cut the backing cloth the same size as the printed block. Use a white or off-white colour, as darker shades may show through the background cloth and make the design look grey or grubby. Remember to pre-wash the backing fabric as well.

RIBBONS

Embroiderers have a wonderful variety of pure silk ribbons in a range of colours, widths and textures to choose from. For the most part, you will be using the 2 mm, 4 mm and 7 mm pure silk ribbons. The ribbons used in this book are from Di van Niekerk's hand-painted range of ribbons, available from needlecraft suppliers and specialty mail-order companies worldwide; visit www.dicraft.co.za for details of your nearest supplier or website. You can substitute with ribbon that you may have in your own collection but check that these are colourfast before you start. Pure silk ribbon, especially the hand-painted, shaded variety, is without doubt the best to use if you want to create a true reflection of nature's plants. It is a soft, pliable ribbon and the changes in shade and colour create an authentic image consistent with that of real flowers and leaves. The plain or solid silk ribbons can also be used in combination with these to cut down on costs, but do bear in mind that if only plain colours are used, the design may be flat and lack depth.

Working with ribbon

Silk ribbon embroidery is surprisingly easy to master. In essence, ribbon is worked just like any thread or yarn – it is just much softer and more fragile. It is vital that you use a large needle with a large enough eye to make a big enough hole in the fabric to prevent the ribbon from snagging and scrunching up as you pull it through the fabric (see Needles on page 27).

Threading ribbon

Thread the needle and pierce the end that has just been threaded. Pull the long tail to tighten the knot. This way the ribbon does not unthread and you can use it almost to the end of the length ensuring less wastage (see Threading ribbon on page 58).

Starting ribbon: You have a number of choices

- Make a looped knot: gather the long end of the ribbon by piercing it once or twice with the threaded needle. Pull the needle and the ribbon all the way through to form a looped knot.

- Leave a small tail at the back and as you make your first or second stitch, pierce the tail to secure the ribbon in place.
- Secure the tail with embroidery thread.
- Knot the narrow 2 mm ribbons (as you would a thread) but only if the texture of the design is busy enough to hide the bulkiness of the knot.

Finishing ribbon: You also have options

- Leave a 1 to 2 cm (³/₈ to ³/₄ in.) tail at the back of the work; secure with one or two strands of embroidery thread.
- Catch the tail when you start your next stitch.
- Weave the ribbon in and out of adjacent stitches at the back.

Choosing different widths

The silk ribbons used in this book are 2 mm, 4 mm and 7 mm wide. I specified the widths I used in the step-by-step instructions. Always take note of the proportions of the design to create a visually pleasing picture; look at the completed design in the book and study the size of a flower in relation to the adjoining shapes. If your flower is too large in comparison, you may struggle creating the correct depth. Let the design guide your choice of ribbon width; observe the size of the flowers and leaves – larger flowers and leaves require wider ribbons; smaller flowers, stems and leaves are best made in 2 mm ribbon. Depending on the stitch you are using, the ribbon should cover all or most of the painted detail without being so large that the flower (or leaf) appears overbearing.

If you are making a smaller initial or picture than the one in the book, use a narrower ribbon: instead of 7 mm use 4 mm; in place of 4 mm ribbon use 2 mm.

HINTS FOR SILK RIBBON EMBROIDERY

- Use short 30 cm (12 in.) lengths, especially with the 7 mm silk ribbons. For the narrow, 2 mm ribbons, use 40 to 45 cm (16 to 18 in.) as this ribbon does not fray as quickly as the wider ribbons. A good rule is to cut a length from the tip of your finger to your elbow; any longer than this makes the ribbon (or thread) difficult to work with.
- Always use a large chenille needle so that the hole is big enough to pull the ribbon through without damaging it (see needles, page 27).
- Cut ribbon at an angle to form a sharp point; it is easier to thread this way.

- Use your left thumb (or right thumb if you're left handed) to hold the ribbon flat as you pull it through to the back. Only let go once the stitch is almost done; this prevents the ribbon from twisting or scrunching up. Alternatively, use the blunt end of a spare tapestry needle to gently hold the ribbon flat until you have pulled it through.
- Work with a gentle tension: ribbon needs to be handled lightly. Keep stitches loose and unfolded; allow the ribbon to spread to its full width on the fabric before starting the next stitch. If your tension is too tight, or the needle is too small, the ribbon will fold or scrunch up and the beautiful texture will be lost.
- When you (inadvertently) pull a stitch too tight, or you don't like the shape of the stitch, don't be deterred; simply make another stitch on top of it – this will add texture to the design. Another trick is to use needle and thread to re-shape the stitch with tiny stab stitches along the edge of the ribbon to coax the stitch into a pleasing shape.
- Some stitches look good if the ribbon twists while you stitch; some are better worked with flat ribbon. Try both and see what works for you.
- The ribbon on a chenille needle will make holes in the fabric for some stitches such as straight stitch and others. When this happens, use one strand of thread and stab stitches to cover the hole and to add texture at the same time.

THREADS

Many different kinds of threads have been used in this book. The brand names and codes have been included for easy reference. If you would like to substitute brands for others, use the designs in the book as a guideline and match the colours with threads you may already have. Just about any thread can be used, as long as you are able to thread it and insert it through the fabric. Check that your threads are colourfast before embroidering your design. The following threads were used for the projects in this book:

STRANDED COTTON
It consists of six strands of fine cotton thread that are easily separated. DMC stranded cotton has a wonderful sheen and the colours can be combined to achieve a shaded effect. Stranded cotton is also available as a space-dyed thread, for example from Chameleon Threads.

RAYON
This is made from naturally occurring polymers in green plants and is therefore neither a synthetic nor a natural fibre. Known as viscose rayon or art silk in the textile trade, it is very smooth and shiny and ideal for filling in initials in couching, chain or stem stitch. Owing to rayon's natural bounce it makes gorgeous, loose, looped French knots. In this book I used rayon from the Chameleon Threads range, as well as the Rajmahal Art.Silk threads which are 65% viscose rayon and 35% silk.

PERLÉ THREAD
A twisted cotton or silk thread with a pearly finish, perlé thread cannot be divided. A raised pattern is achieved with this thread and it is ideal for raised stem-stitch, as shown in the initial C on pages 33 and 64, or satin couching, as used in the initial L on pages 35 and 82. The finer no 12 or medium no 8 perlé cotton thread is available from DMC and Chameleon Threads. Perlé silk thread is available from Gumnut yarns in Australia.

PURE SILK
Silk thread has a lustrous, rich texture and is surprisingly easy to work with. It is produced from the cocoons of silkworms. Depending on the brand, the thread consists of 4, 6, 7, 8 or 12 individual strands. In this book I recommend using one or two strands, but do experiment with more strands on your needle to find a texture that suits you. For couching, the threads are not divided at all (see couching on page 34). I used stranded silks from Chameleon Threads and Gumnut Yarns.

METALLIC THREADS
These are available in one strand or six. This thread adds a touch of glamour to your design and highlights detail beautifully. Use short lengths and a needle with a medium eye to gently pull the thread through the fabric without damaging the beautiful sheen. I used the Madeira and DMC Metallic threads.

Starting a thread
There are several ways to do this.
- Make a knot at the long end and use a waste knot: start a short distance away, somewhere on a leaf or flower that will later be covered with stitches; insert the needle from the front to the back. Come up on the section that you wish to embroider and make a few small back stitches; cover these back stitches as you work the piece. Cut the waste knot away once the section has been stitched.

- Make a knot at the long end; come up from the back. This method is useful when stitching a denser section on the design where the knot will not be visible once stitched.
- When couching with six strands of thread, it is better not to use a waste knot as a hole will be visible in the fabric once it is cut away; rather use a knot coming up from the back, or lay the six strands on top of your work and as you start, use one strand of thread and several couching stitches overlapping each other to secure the six strands to the design.

Finishing a thread

End off by weaving the thread in and out of adjacent stitches at the back, or use several tiny stab stitches on a section of a flower or leaf that will be covered with stitches later.

NEEDLES

Using the correct size needle is probably the most important factor determining a successful project. Many an embroiderer is surprised by the large size of needles required for ribbon embroidery. It is vital that the needle makes a large enough hole in the fabric so that the ribbon is pulled through gently without

snagging or hurting the silk. The ribbon spreads evenly to form a soft, open stitch, instead of being all scrunched up when pulled through too small a hole. The eye of the needle must also be long enough for the ribbon to lie flat once it is threaded. You will need only four needle types for this kind of embroidery:

CHENILLE

A sharp-pointed, thick needle with a large eye. Use a size 18 (large) for the 7 mm ribbon, size 20 (medium) for the 4 mm ribbon and 22 or 24 (fine) for the 2 mm ribbon and perlé thread. In a mixed pack of 18/24 chenille needles, the largest needle is a size 18.

CREWEL/EMBROIDERY

A sharp, fine needle with a long, large eye. Use size 5 to 7 for perlé cotton, rayon and three to six strands of thread; use a size 8 to 9 for one or two strands of thread and metallic thread, and a size 10 for beading. In a mixed pack of 5/10 crewel needles, the largest needle is a size 5.

STRAW/MILLINERS

A long, sharp needle with a small eye no wider than the shaft. This is the only needle to use for bullion knots. The wraps slip off the needle easily as the eye is not too wide. In a mixed pack of 3/9 straw/milliner's needles, the largest needle is a size 3 which is useful for working with perlé thread. The finest size 9 needle is good for beading – stronger than a beading needle and fine enough to fit through the smallest bead.

TAPESTRY

A thick needle with a large eye and a blunt point. It is useful for whipped chain or back stitch and for coaxing stitches into shape – the blunt point prevents you from damaging the ribbon by mistake. A mixed pack of size 18/24 is handy and a large size 13 or 16 tapestry needle is a good choice for working over when forming loose/puffed ribbon stitches.

EMBROIDERY FRAMES OR HOOPS

Always use a large enough hoop to accommodate the full design. This way, the edges of the hoop won't damage the stitches and you are able to see the entire design as you work; this helps with choice of colour and texture. All the stab stitches (stitches made through the fabric) are best embroidered on the hoop, especially satin stitch, French knots, stem-stitch filling and couching – the stretched layers prevent the design from puckering out of shape. Some of the surface stitches such as chain and stem stitch can be stitched off the hoop. Some embroiderers prefer to do stem stitch on the hoop, stab-stitch style. This is very much a personal choice – see what works for you.

To prevent the hoop from stretching and marking the fabric, bind the inner frame with strips of sheeting or bias-binding first, to hold the fabric comfortably. Secure in place with a few stitches. Hoop stands that hold the hoop so that both your hands are free, are available from needlecraft stores. If you have chosen not to use a 'window' cloth on top of your work (see Keeping your work clean, page 29), remove or at least loosen your work from the hoop when you are not working on it; the hoop does tend to leave a dirty mark around the edge. Every now and then, pull the fabric taut in the hoop as you stitch; tighten the screw as often as necessary for a smooth, professional finish. Roll up the four corners outside the hoop and pin or tack them in place – this way, the fabric will not get in the way you as you stitch.

OTHER REQUIREMENTS

I have not listed everything you may need as each project is different. Treat the following as a guide only – you do not need all these items for a successful project.

- Small embroidery scissors with sharp points are a must.
- You may also need pins, pincushion, needle case, tacking cotton for rolled up corners.
- A needle threader and needle grabber (a small piece of rubber to help pull the needle through).
- Keep wet-wipes or a damp cloth close by for clean hands.
- A floss box (plastic compartmentalized container) is handy to store threads: wind threads onto thread bobbins and ribbon onto soft cardboard rolls.
- A large fabric bag or pillow case to store your embroidery.
- A rubber, leather or steel thimble.
- Daylight or a good light.
- A comfortable chair and worktable, if possible, so that all your ribbons, threads and tools are within easy reach – this way you can also rest the hoop on the edge of the table as you work.
- A pledge to have more *me-time;* embroidery is probably the best way to make you slow down, taking a creative break from the frantic pressures of our modern way of life.

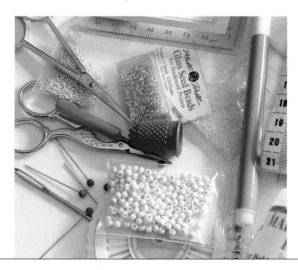

KEEPING YOUR WORK CLEAN

To keep your embroidery clean, use the window method. Cut a block of inexpensive white fabric the same size as your embroidery cloth. Place the hoop that you will be using on top of this fabric; use a pencil to draw a circle 2,5 to 5 cm (1 to 2 in.) inside the rim of the hoop: the circle is smaller than the hoop. Cut out along the drawn circle to make a 'window' in the fabric. Place the embroidery cloth right side up over the backing fabric. Place the 'window cloth' over your embroidery cloth: this prevents the edges of the embroidery from becoming dirty. You can also use a sheet of plastic-wrap (also known as cling-film or cling-wrap) or a sheet of tissue paper instead of fabric. Insert all three layers in the hoop to make a 'sandwich', stretching it as taut as a drum. Check that the backing fabric is wrinkle free as well and tighten the hoop. Roll up the corners of the fabric and pin or tack out of the way to prevent you from stitching the corners onto the back of the work by mistake.

Washing instructions

Depending on the transfer method you have used, follow the manufacturer's instructions for washing the background fabric. The following are guidelines only: Designs printed with heat transfer sheets should be washed in cold water; use a gentle detergent such as soap flakes or mild soap for delicate fabrics – don't use any bleach or harsh detergents. Don't allow to soak, but wash and hang up to dry. Whilst still damp, press with an iron set to the appropriate temperature for the fabric. Don't iron directly on the printed area; cover the printed image with a sheet of regular white paper or a Teflon® sheet. This also helps to brighten the colours of the transfer.

Don't press on the embroidered section and always iron on the wrong side using several layers of sheeting on the ironing board to protect the embroidered stitches.

USEFUL HINTS

- Refer to the colour photograph of the embroidered initial or the watercolour of the painted initial whilst stitching, especially for stems and leaves; these may well have been covered by stitches (that you have already made) and you could fail to notice them.
- Use the best quality fabric, ribbons and threads you can afford to ensure an heirloom quality project.
- Keep the embroidery stretched taut in a hoop as you work to ensure a perfect tension; tighten each time you start stitching to ensure a smooth finish.
- Never store fabrics in plastic; they will sweat and discolour – rather wrap them in an old sheet or a pillowcase. Don't fold the printed or embroidered cloths; store them flat or gently rolled up.
- Keep framed embroideries away from direct sunlight or harsh lights to prevent fading.
- Change your needles regularly; they do tend to become blunt after continued use.
- Don't be deterred by imperfections in your work; the designs are detailed enough to hide most 'mistakes'. Unpick only if it is absolutely necessary; rather make more stitches on top of the ones you don't like – this adds texture to your design; the charm of your design may be lost if it looks too perfect.

Stitches and techniques

Stitches that are made through the fabric are easier to embroider **stab-stitch style**, on a hoop, with the fabric stretched tautly, to prevent your piece from puckering out of shape – these are primarily satin stitch, straight/stab stitch, couching, French knots and stem-stitch filling. For these stitches it is better to take the needle to the back first, and then to come up again, in two separate steps.

I find it is a good idea to make all the stitches on the hoop stab-stitch style; this is very much a personal choice – see what works for you. Remember to tighten the layers in the hoop often so that the cloth does not pucker; gently pull all the layers on each corner and tighten the screw.

Some of the surface stitches such as chain and stem stitch can be stitched without a hoop, in your hand.

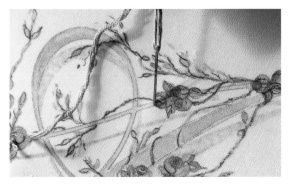

Stab-stitch – take the needle to the back, then come up again in two separate steps.

Embroidery off the hoop

FILLING IN A MONOGRAM/INITIAL OF A WORD

The ornately painted initials on pages 121 to 125 are used to form the main part of a monogram, or the first letter of a word, name or sentence. The embroidery of each initial is described step-by-step on pages 60 to 111. The initials are embroidered in several ways, using various stitches to create different textures.

Depending on how much time you wish to spend on your project, choose the stitch that you. In this book I used seven stitches to embroider the initials before adding the flowers, leaves and other embellishments.

Outline only in back stitch

The initials have been painted in watercolour for you to embellish with flowers, stems and leaves. It is not necessary to always fill in the initial; use the colour print to do some of the work for you and only outline the initial in back stitch. This will highlight the initial and give it an edge. Choose a contrasting thread such as a medium grey, green or any complementary colour. One strand of thread is advised for this stitch (see back stitch, page 53).

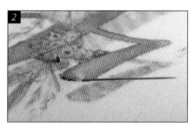
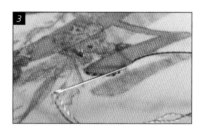
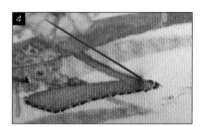

Stem-stitch filling

Stem-stitch filling has a smooth, textured finish. After making a waste knot and a few back stitches to anchor the thread, work on the outer edge, at the tip of the initial, and work row after row of stem stitch close together for a raised effect. Use rayon or silk thread for a shiny appearance and cotton thread for a matt finish. One or two strands of thread are ideal (see stem-stitch filling on page 57).

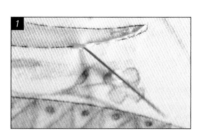
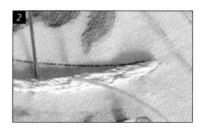

Buttonhole quarter-wheel

Use buttonhole or blanket stitch to create quarter-wheel wedges. To start, come up on the outer edge of the initial; insert the needle into the same hole each time you make a stitch to form the wedge shape. The stitches can be made close together (buttonhole stitch) or further apart (blanket stitch). Use one strand of silk or cotton thread for maximum effect (see buttonhole stitch: quarter-wheel, page 53).

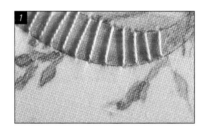
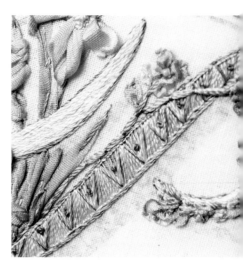

Raised stem-stitch

This stitch has a lovely raised texture. The initial will have a rough texture if you use perlé no 12 thread, or a fine texture if worked in silk thread. Work this stitch on the hoop to prevent the fabric from puckering out of shape, and space the foundation spokes evenly apart. When forming the raised stem-stitches, push each row towards the previous one, using the nail of your index finger so that the rows are tucked close together. By pushing the rows close together a rounded texture will be achieved (see raised stem-stitch, page 55).

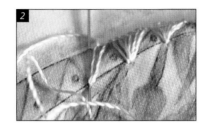
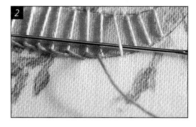

Couching

Couching full strands of cotton, silk, or rayon, without dividing or separating the threads, creates an interesting, rippled texture. For the laid thread (the thread that will be couched in place) use pure silk, six-stranded cotton or rayon, or one strand of perlé no 8 thread. Cut a long length for the laid thread and use one strand of a matching cotton or silk thread (normal length) to secure the laid thread in place. Start on the edge of the initial or flower and work towards the centre until the initial is filled. Space the stitches about 3 to 4 mm ($^1/_8$ in.) apart. Retain an even tension on the long, laid thread, pulling it gently as you couch it in place to ensure a smooth finish. The couching stitches are neater if you come up close to, or underneath the laid thread; work over the laid thread and insert the needle back into the same hole – this way the stitch fits snugly and neatly around the couched thread. Take the threads to the back and end off (see couching, page 53).

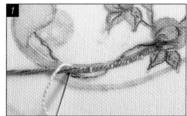

HINT

When working with two needles, always ensure that one of the needles are on top of your work. If you have both needles dangling at the back, the threads will become entangled.

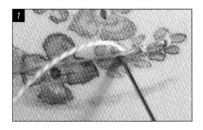

Satin couching

Use satin couching for a smooth, raised initial: couch perlé no 8 or six strands of cotton thread in place (see couching opposite and on page 53). Couch the rows close together; make a few more rows on top of the first layer, especially towards

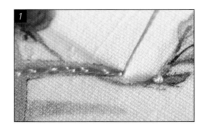
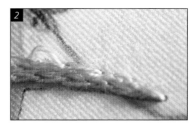

the centre of the initial. By stitching two (or even three) layers on top of one another, the initial will be nicely rounded. Thread up with one strand of silk thread (or rayon for more shine) and use satin stitch to cover the couched threads. Work perpendicular (at right angles) to

the couched thread and use a gentle, even tension for a smooth finish. Angle the needle under the couched threads to 'tuck them in' for a smooth edge (see satin couching on page 56). Work a row of chain stitch along the edge to neaten it and to highlight it at the same time.

Chain-stitch filling

This is row upon row of chain stitches made close together. When using one strand of silk or rayon thread, a lovely, soft, yet raised texture is achieved. This stitch can be worked in the hand (off the hoop) but take care that the background fabric does not pucker. Use a gentle, even tension to prevent wrinkling. Work from the outer edge towards the centre. Once the initial is filled in, use a strand of a contrasting thread such as a medium grey or green and work a row of stem stitch along the edge to create a neat outline (see chain-stitch filling on page 53).

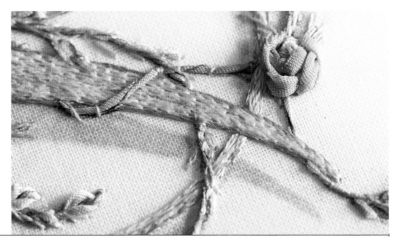

EMBELLISHING THE INITIALS

The initials can be embellished with various flowers and shapes.

Daisy-like flowers and old-fashioned dog roses

Ribbon stitch was used for the blue petals and a yellow bead was added in the centre. Use a gentle tension whilst forming each petal. See loose/puffed ribbon stitch in the stitch gallery on page 55.

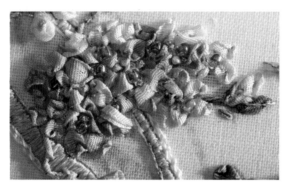

In this example, light pink ribbon is used for the pale pink flowers and dark pink ribbon for the darker pink flowers. Form each petal in loose/puffed ribbon stitch working over a spare tapestry needle to raise the stitches off the surface of the design. Work from the centre outwards, overlapping some petals for a dense texture. Add a pink or lavender bead in the centre of each flower. Use green ribbon and loose/puffed ribbon stitches to form the green leaves between the pink flowers.

Ribbon stitch was used for the daisy petals. Note how the stitch lies quite flat on the fabric (not loose and puffed) and the stitches overlap each other in places. Add a cluster of French knots in the centre of the daisy. See ribbon stitch on page 55.

Here detached chain-stitch was used for some petals and ribbon stitch for others. Add a French knot at the tip of the ribbon stitches and make a cluster of French knots in the centre.

For tiny daisies, use 2 mm silk ribbon and work over the stitches on the initial. Use straight stitch to form narrow, pointed petals and ribbon stitch to form a slightly wider petal with a rounded tip. Alternate between the two stitches for an interesting effect and add a yellow bead in the centre of each daisy. See attaching a bead on page 38 and straight stitch on page 58.

For large petals, use 7 mm silk ribbon and loop stitch. See loop stitch on page 55. Work over a spare tapestry needle as you form the loops, stitching from the centre outwards. For the smaller flowers use loose and puffed ribbon stitch. Change to a yellow thread and make tiny stab stitches in the centre of the flower. Add a blue bead in the centre of the flower. See stab stitch on page 57.

Here detached chain-stitch was used for each petal. Work from the centre outwards and add a black French knot or bead in the centre. See detached chain/lazy daisy stitch on page 53 and French knot on page 54.

To create curled-up petals for the cosmos in the G initial, work ribbon stitch with curled-up tips. Insert a spare tapestry needle into the loop that is formed as you take the ribbon to the back of your work. See ribbon stitch with curled-up tips in the stitch gallery on page 56.

For old-fashioned roses, ribbon stitches with curled-up tips always look good. Work from the centre outwards to create the flower and make clusters of French knots in the centre of the rose.

Here ribbon stitch with curled-up tips was used for the pink dog roses. The stitches overlap for a dense texture. Use a darker pink thread and make a French knot in the centre.

Round shapes or clusters of small flowers

Loop stitch is ideal for clusters of small flowers. Work over a spare tapestry needle and form one loop stitch for each flower. Use a matching thread and make a French knot on top of each loop to form the centre of the flower. See loop stitch with a French knot centre on page 55.

For these small flowers use 7 mm silk ribbon and a loop stitch. Change to lilac thread and add two French knots on top of each loop, wrapping the thread twice around the needle. See loop stitch with a French knot centre on page 55.

French knots are ideal for round shapes. Large shapes are made with silk ribbon wrapped loosely two or three times around the needle. Wrap the thread once around the needle for smaller dots, two or three times around the needle for larger dots. See French knot on page 54.

Attaching a bead: Beads are also a good choice for round shapes or clusters. Secure in place with one strand of thread; use three stitches for each bead, inserting the needle into the bead each time.

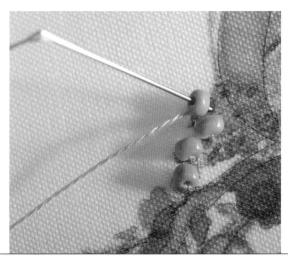

Buds and tiny flowers

Rose buds are usually shaped like teardrops and detached chain-stitch is a good choice. Work from the stem outwards. See detached chain/lazy daisy stitch on page 53.

For this bud, detached chain-stitch was used. To make a narrow base use blue thread and a grab stitch. See grab stitch in the stitch gallery on page 54. The green calyx is formed with 2 mm silk ribbon and a fly stitch. See fly stitch on page 54.

For this bud, the dark orange section is made in detached chain-stitch. Use a lighter shade of yellow or orange ribbon and make a ribbon stitch in the centre of the chain stitch. Change to brown or green thread and make a few straight stitches on top of the bud for a realistic finish. The tiny orange buds are made in straight stitch. See straight stitch on page 58.

Here the lavender blue buds were made with ribbon stitch. To form the round pink bud at the tip of the lavender bud, use silk ribbon and a one-wrap French knot. The remaining pink buds are made in straight stitch.

Roses

Spider-web roses are quick and easy to make. Use a green or matching thread and make five foundation spokes. Wrap the needle and ribbon under and over each spoke using a gentle tension for a life-like rose. See spiderweb rose in the stitch gallery on page 57. When roses are closely packed alongside each other, insert the needle under adjoining stitches if the foundation spokes are no longer visible. Add one or several golden yellow French knots or beads in the centre of the rose.

SPIDERWEB ROSES

The five foundation spokes are made with green thread, the rose with 4 mm silk ribbon. Use a gentle, even tension for a soft, open rose. Use a few green or golden yellow French knots to form the dark centre of the rose. See spiderweb rose on page 57.

FLY-STITCH ROSE

Make a three-wrap French knot to form the centre of the rose. Use 4 mm silk ribbon to make two or three fly stitches alongside each other. See fly-stitch rose in the stitch gallery on page 54.

FLY-STITCH ROSE

Here 2 mm pink silk ribbon and three French knots are used to form the pink centre. Then 4 mm silk ribbon is used to make a fly-stitch rose around the pink centre.

FLY- AND RIBBON-STITCH ROSE

Use two strands of pink thread; make a three-wrap French knot to form the pink centre of the rose. Use 4 mm silk ribbon and make two or three fly stitches close together. Add one or two ribbon stitches at the base of the rose to form the open petals. Use the pink thread again; add more French knots in the centre if necessary. See fly-stitch rose and fly- and ribbon-stitch rose in the stitch gallery on page 54.

STEM-STITCH ROSE

Use a golden yellow 2 mm silk ribbon, form the centre with a three-wrap French knot. Change to 4 mm silk ribbon and use loosely formed stem stitches to make the rose petals. Use a gentle tension so as not to flatten the stitches. See stem-stitch rose in the stitch gallery on page 57.

RIBBON-STITCH ROSE

Form the centre first with golden yellow thread and three French knots (wrap thread three times around the needle). Use a dark orange 4 mm silk ribbon and starting close to the French knots make ribbon stitches to form the petals of the rose. Use a gentle tension and work over a spare tapestry needle to form loose/puffed ribbon stitches. See ribbon-stitch rose on page 56 and loose/puffed ribbon stitch on page 55. Change to a lighter orange ribbon and make a few ribbon stitches on top of the others to form the light orange petals.

Berries, grapes and tiny flowers

For berries or grapes, use small glass seed beads. See attaching a bead on page 38. An alternative stitch for berries and grapes is a French knot made in thread or silk ribbon.

For tiny round flowers, use a glass seed bead or French knot made in ribbon or thread.

Tiny flowers at the end of or branching off the stem are made in ribbon or straight stitch. Use ribbon for the wider flowers and thread for the tiny shapes. The same applies to the leaves at the end of or branching off the stem.

Irises

Use 4 mm silk ribbon for small irises, 7 mm silk ribbon for larger irises. Make the top upright section first. Work from the centre of the iris upwards and use one detached chain-stitch in the centre. Add one or two ribbon stitches alongside to fill in the shape of the upright petals. Form the bottom section in detached chain-stitch and work from the centre downwards. Make the two side petals in ribbon stitch. Work from the centre outwards. Use one strand of yellow thread and make several French knots in the centre of the iris.

Pansies

Use 7 mm silk ribbon for small pansies, 13 mm for larger pansies and work from the centre outwards. Form the five petals in ribbon stitch. Use ribbon or thread and form the stripes on the petals in straight stitch. Add a bead or French knot in the centre of the pansy.

Butterfly

Make the body first. Use a grey or brown silky thread and whipped back-stitch. Make the four wings in padded ribbon-stitch (see padded ribbon-stitch in the stitch gallery on page 55). Work from the body outwards. Change to white metallic thread and add a few straight or pistil stitches at the base of each wing. Make the antennae with a pistil stitch. See pistil stitch on page 55.

Stems

THICK STEMS

Use two strands of green thread and start at the thick base of the stem with chain stitch. Each chain is about 5 mm (³/₁₆ in.) long. End off and start at the base again, completing all the stems in chain stitch. Use a green silk ribbon and whip the chain stitch to form a life-like stem. At the thick base of the stem insert the needle under all the rows of chain stitch at the same time. For the thin stems, insert the needle under and over the single row of chain stitch. See whipped chain-stitch on page 58.

A quicker way of making *thick stems*: use whipped back-stitch instead of whipped chain-stitch. Make two rows of back stitch on either side of the stem and whip with 2 or 4 mm silk ribbon, inserting the needle under both rows of stitches at the same time. See whipped back-stitch: double row on page 58.

Here the thick rose stem was filled in with rows of couching using all six strands of thread. The thin stems are made with a single row of couching.

THIN STEMS

Use couching, back, stem, or chain stitch for the foundation row and whip the stitches with ribbon or thread. Use straight stitch in silk ribbon or thread for the very fine stalks at the end of the stems. See page 58 for various whipped stitches.

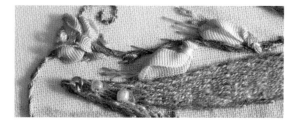

Here the *thin stems* are made in back stitch, whipped with silk ribbon. See whipped back-stitch on page 58.

Here the *thin stems* are made in back stitch, whipped with thread. See whipped back-stitch on page 58.

To form *thin, twirled stems*, use silk ribbon and twist the ribbon before couching it in place with a matching thread. Use a gentle tension to avoid flattening the ribbon.

Fine stems are also made in straight stitch. Use ribbon or thread. See straight stitch on page 58.

Decorating a stem

To add more colour, use a contrasting thread and whip the stem yet again. Use a gentle tension to avoid flattening the stem.

Leaves

Use fly stitch for *large leaves*. See fly stitch on page 54.

For *small leaves* use straight stitch. Use thread for very fine leaves and ribbon for larger ones.

Or detached chain-stitch. Use a long anchoring stitch for *long leaves*.

For *medium size leaves* use ribbon stitch. Use a contrasting thread and a stab stitch at the tip of the leaves to add colour and to secure the stitch at the same time.

For *straight or upright leaves* use twisted ribbon or twisted straight-stitch. See twisted stitches on page 58.

Outlining a shape

For outlining shapes like hearts or circles, use silk ribbon and a whipped back or chain stitch. See whipped back and whipped chain-stitch on page 58. Whipped stem or couching is also a good choice. See page 58.

Decorating the letter

Use French knots to add interesting detail to an embroidered initial. See French knot on page 54.

Use a contrasting thread and straight stitch to make interesting patterns. Add French knots between the stitches for texture. See straight stitch on page 58.

Use gold or silver metallic thread and stem or back stitch along the edge of the initial for interesting highlights.

Use different colours to create a pattern. Here buttonhole stitch is used for the pink and yellow triangles, straight stitch for the blue zigzag pattern, and blue French knots are added on the pink triangles for texture. See buttonhole stitch: quarter wheel on page 53.

Use French knots on top of the embroidered initial in matching thread to create a subtle texture.

EMBROIDERING LETTERS OF A WORD

Words are filled in whipped back-stitch. Fill in the letter with back stitch: use silk ribbon for larger words and thread for smaller letters. Whip the back stitch with silk ribbon or thread. Insert the needle under and over the foundation stitches, use an even tension for good results. Whipped chain-stitch is a good alternative, as is whipped stem-stitch. See various whipped stitches on page 58.

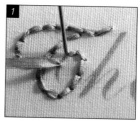
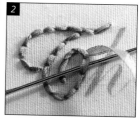

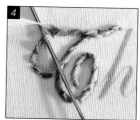

Medium size letters

Here whipped back-stitch in silk ribbon was used to fill in the name.

The C of *Carla* and the L of *Love* were not filled in, just outlined and embellished with ribbon flowers and stems. The letters were filled in with whipped chain-stitch and 4 mm silk ribbon.

It is not always necessary to fill in the letters of the word or initial. For a quick project the embroidered piece used to decorate a towel box for a wedding gift, the C initial was embellished with ribbon roses and stems and the letters of the word were left just printed.

Small letters

The words on these small trinket boxes were stitched in back stitch with thread and whipped with 2 mm silk ribbon. The letters for the *Dina* teddy were slightly larger and therefore 2 mm silk ribbon was used for the back stitch and these were whipped with the same 2 mm ribbon. See whipped back-stitch in the stitch gallery on page 58.

Tiny letters

Here the word *love* was used on a tiny teddy and therefore made in whipped back-stitch with one strand of red thread. The word *angel* was made for a small beanie and here, too, thread was used to fill in the letters.

Large letters

For this embellished T-shirt two rows of back stitch were used to outline the edge of the letters and these were whipped with 4 mm silk ribbon. The needle was inserted under both rows of stitches at the same time. See whipped back-stitch: double row in the stitch gallery on page 58.

Here 2 mm silk ribbon and chain-stitch filling have been used to fill in large letters. See chain-stitch filling on page 53.

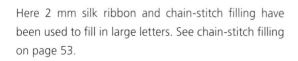

COVERING HOLES

If the needle used for the ribbon leaves a hole in the fabric, use matching (or contrasting) thread and straight stitch to secure the ribbon in place, covering the hole at the same time.

ATTACHING THE EMBROIDERY TO THE PROJECT

Each design is made separately and then applied onto a gift item such as a towel, teddy, handbag, or any other project that you have planned.

For this dream journal, the design was embroidered on a large white cotton block. The journal was first covered with white felt that was glued onto the journal with acid-free fabric glue. The embroidered cloth was used to cover the felted journal, as you would with a schoolbook, glued in place on the inside flaps. Slip stitch was used to secure the corners on the inside flap. Organza ribbon was stitched along the edge of the spine with blanket stitch.

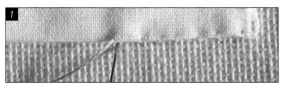

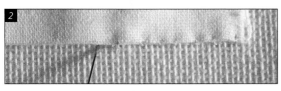

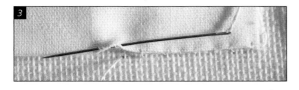

Slip stitch: Use a contrasting or matching thread. Turn the seam to the back of the embroidered cloth and pin the design onto the background. Use a neat slip stitch to secure the cloth onto the background, spacing the stitches about 5 mm (³/₁₆ in.) apart. Come up from the back, catch the edge of the seam and pull the needle and thread all the way through to the front of your work. Insert the needle into the background cloth taking the needle and thread all the way through to the back again. Come up 5 mm (³/₁₆ in.) away and insert the needle into the folded seam, pull the needle and thread all the way through before inserting the needle to the back again. Repeat the process and try to keep the stitches as even as possible for a neat finish.

Slip stitch was used here to secure the embroidered cloth onto a little girl's hat. See the hat on page 59.

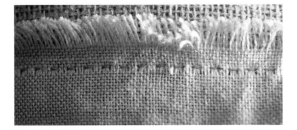

Running stitch was used to secure the design to a Hessian shopping-bag.

Three edges of the embroidered piece were stitched onto a baby beanie in back stitch, the bottom edge in running stitch.

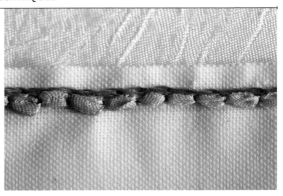

Back stitch was used here to secure the design onto a light background, adding a decorative edge.

Before the design is removed from the hoop, use running or back stitch along a pencil line. This will ensure that the line is straight. Remove from the hoop, cut out the design leaving a small seam. Turn the seam to the back and use a slip stitch to attach it to the background. For a rustic effect, leave a raw edge (don't turn the seam to the back) and use matching thread and stab or running stitch, working along the edge of back stitches to secure the design in place.

Running stitch was used to secure this embroidered Russian word for Cherish to a scarf.

Blanket stitch was used to secure the embroidered name onto a baby's blanket.

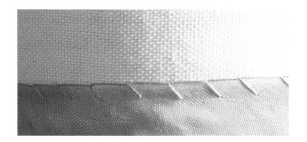

Single feather stitch, similar to blanket stitch but with slanted arms, was used to secure the silk ribbon to the edge of a round box (left).

Blanket stitch was used to decorate the edge of the lid (right). Use 2 or 4 mm silk ribbon and make the first row of blanket stitch along the edge of the lid, inserting the needle into the fabric each time. Make a second row of looped blanket stitches, inserting the needle through the loop of the stitch in the first row. Repeat for a third time using a gentle, even tension for a frilly effect. The only time the needle is inserted into the fabric is when you start and end a row, or the length of ribbon is too short and you have to end off and start again.

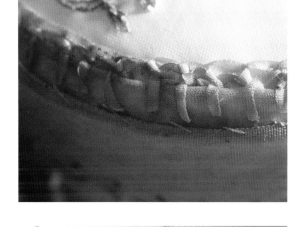

Feather stitch and blue silk ribbon was used to secure the embroidered piece onto this pink hat.

Blanket stitch was used to attach the design to a knitted blanket.

Use *back stitch* along the edge; fray the edge and glue the embroidery to the side of a painted box, using fabric glue.

Make a few pleats in the fabric below the embroidery and use *back stitch* by hand or your sewing machine to secure the embroidery to the edge of a pillow case.

Stitch gallery

The following stitches are illustrated on the next few pages:

1. Back stitch
2. Blanket stitch
3. Buttonhole stitch
4. Buttonhole stitch: quarter wheel
5. Chain stitch
6. Chain-stitch filling
7. Couching
8. Detached chain-stitch/lazy daisy
9. Feather stitch
10. Fly stitch
11. Fly- and ribbon-stitch rose
12. Fly-stitch rose
13. Folded straight-stitch
14. French knot
15. Grab stitch
16. Loop stitch
17. Loop stitch with a French knot centre
18. Loose/puffed ribbon stitch
19. Outline stitch
20. Overcast stitch
21. Padded ribbon-stitch
22. Pistil stitch
23. Ribbon stitch
24. Raised stem-stitch
25. Ribbon stitch: curled-up tips
26. Ribbon-stitch rose
27. Running stitch
28. Satin couching
29. Satin stitch for blocks
30. Satin stitch for leaves
31. Single knotted stitch
32. Split stitch
33. Spiderweb rose
34. Split back-stitch
35. Stab stitch
36. Stem stitch
37. Stem-stitch filling
38. Stem-stitch rose
39. Straight stitch
40. Threading ribbon
41. Twisted ribbon-stitch
42. Twisted straight-stitch
43. Whipped back-stitch
44. Whipped back-stitch: double row
45. Whipped chain-stitch
46. Whipped couching
47. Whipped stem-stitch

1. *Back stitch*

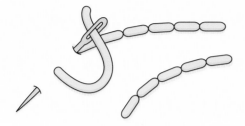

2. *Blanket stitch*

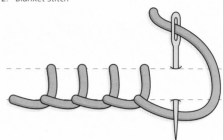

3. *Buttonhole stitch*

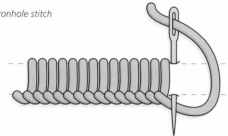

4. *Buttonhole stitch: quarter wheel*

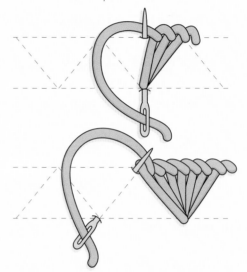

5. *Chain stitch*

6. *Chain-stitch filling*

7. *Couching*

8. *Detached chain-stitch/lazy daisy*

9. *Feather stitch*

10. *Fly stitch*

11. *Fly- and ribbon-stitch rose*

12. *Fly-stitch rose*

13. *Folded straight-stitch*

14. *French knot*

15. *Grab stitch*

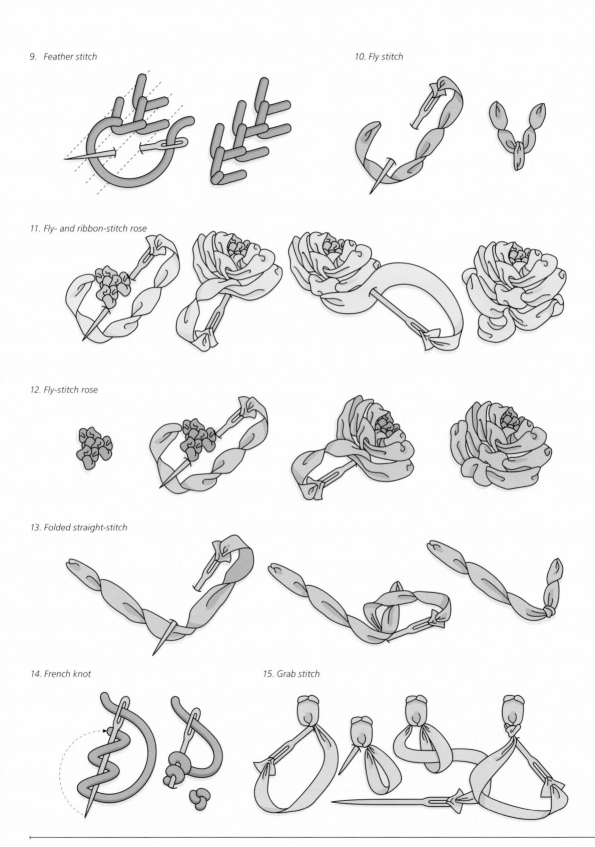

16. Loop stitch

17. Loop stitch with a French knot centre

18. Loose/puffed ribbon stitch

19. Outline stitch

20. Overcast stitch

21. Padded ribbon-stitch

22. Pistil stitch

23. Ribbon stitch

24. Raised stem-stitch

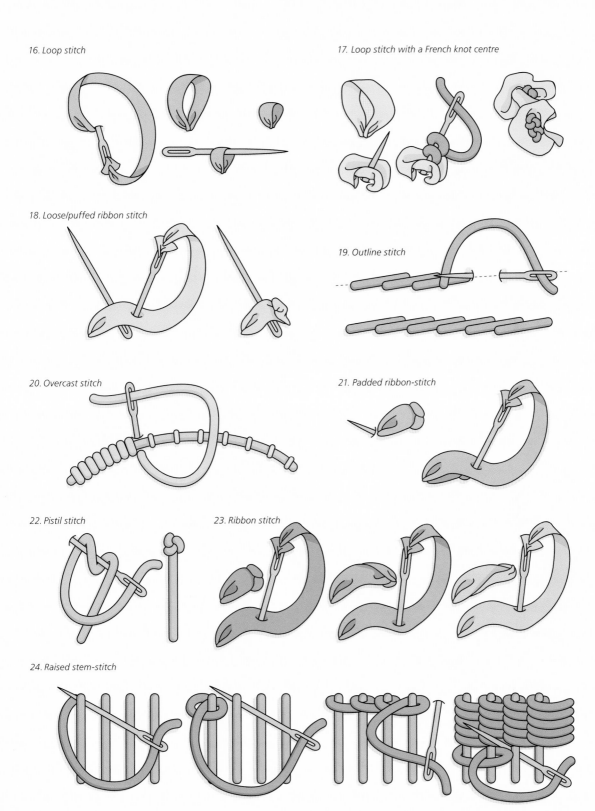

25. Ribbon stitch: curled-up tips

26. Ribbon-stitch rose

27. Running stitch

28. Satin couching

29. Satin stitch for blocks

30. Satin stitch for leaves

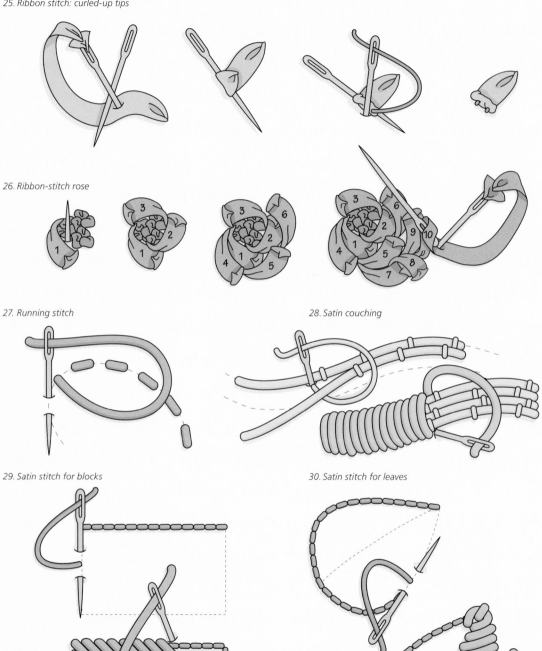

31. Single knotted stitch

32. Split stitch

33. Spiderweb rose

34. Split back-stitch

35. Stab stitch

36. Stem stitch

37. Stem-stitch filling

38. Stem-stitch rose

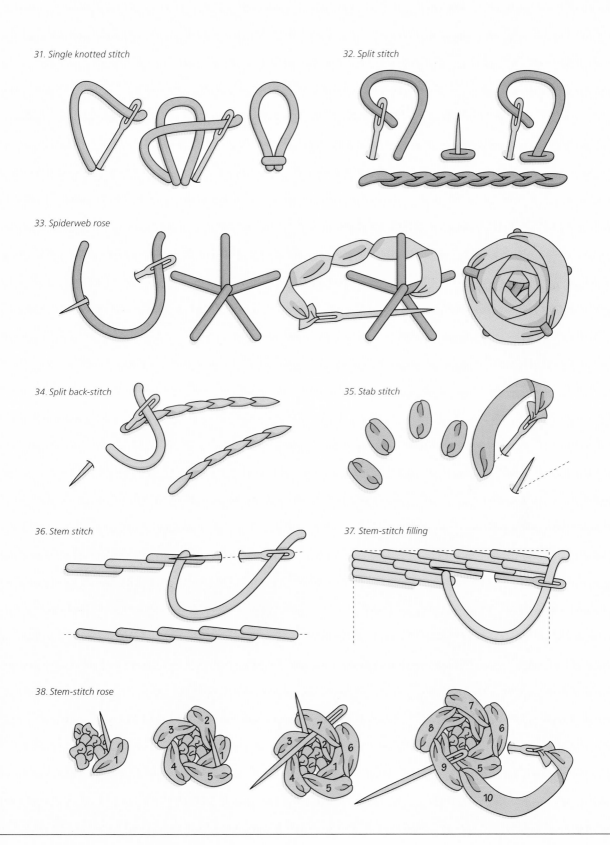

39. Straight stitch

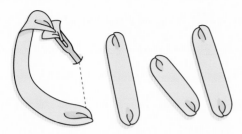

40. Threading ribbon

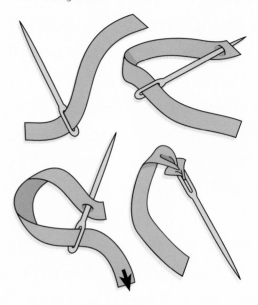

41. Twisted ribbon-stitch

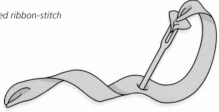

42. Twisted straight-stitch

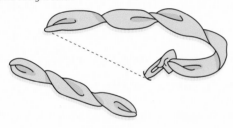

43. Whipped back-stitch

44. Whipped back-stitch: double row

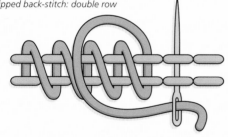

45. Whipped chain-stitch

46. Whipped couching

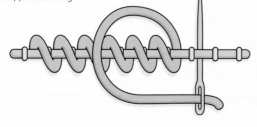

47. Whipped stem-stitch

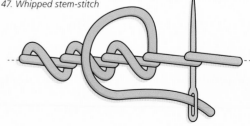

The alphabet: ornate letters

1. Fill in the initial: Use all six strands and a 4 m length of thread **a** for the laid thread, and couch this thread in place with one strand (normal length) of a matching thread **a**. Space the stitches about 3 to 4 mm (¹/₈ in.) apart. Work rows alongside each other and fill in the initial. See more about couching on page 34.

2. Make the stems: Start at the thick base of the stem, couch all six strands of thread **b**, work up to the pink rose at the top of the initial. Proceed down to the tip of the stem at A and end off. Start at the thick base again, work over the first rose, twirling the stem around the initial. Start at the thick base again and complete all the stems this way.

3. Make the small leaves: Use ribbon **1** and straight stitch for the straight leaves. Work from the stem outwards. For tiny round leaves use a two-wrap French knot.

4. Make the large leaves: Use ribbon **1** and detached chain-stitch for the larger leaves.

THREAD

▮▮▮▮▮▮▮▮▮ a) Gumnut Aztecs sapphire (medium)

▮▮▮▮▮▮▮▮▮ b) Chameleon stranded cotton no. 6

▮▮▮▮▮▮▮▮▮ c) DMC precious metal effects E677

Note: use one strand of thread unless suggested otherwise.

RIBBONS

▮▮▮▮▮▮▮▮▮ 1) Di van Niekerk's 2mm silk no. 19

▮▮▮▮▮▮▮▮▮ 2) Di van Niekerk's 4mm silk no. 45

NEEDLES

Crewel size 7 and 9; Chenille size 20 and 22; Tapestry size 20

WHAT ELSE?

- printed or traced design
- backing fabric
- window fabric
- 10 inch (25 cm) hoop

STITCHES USED (SEE STITCH GALLERY PAGES 52-58)

Couching; Detached chain-stitch; Fly stitch; French knot; Grab stitch; Outline stitch; Ribbon stitch; Spiderweb rose; Stem stitch; Straight stitch; Whipped couching

TO REFRESH YOUR MEMORY

- Before you start *pages 23-28*
- Keeping your work clean and useful hints *page 29*
- Stitches and techniques *pages 31-49*

5. Make the pink buds: Use ribbon **2** and straight stitch for the tiny buds, ribbon stitch for the larger, open buds. Use ribbon **1** and a fly or grab stitch to form the green calyx at the base of the bud.

6. Make the pink roses: Use ribbon **2** and make spiderweb roses. Use thread **b** to form the five foundation spokes. Use thread **b** to add three French knots in the centre of the completed rose. Wrap thread three times around the needle.

7. Embellish the initial: Use thread **c** and whip the stems, inserting the needle under and over the stem to add golden highlights. Add a straight stitch at the tip of the small buds and leaves. Outline the left edge of the curved part of the initial in stem or outline stitch.

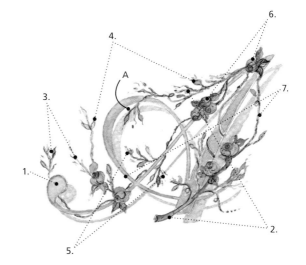

1. Fill in the initial: Use two strands of thread **a** and form the foundation stitches for raised stem-stitch. Work horizontal stitches from side to side and space them about 3 mm (1/8 in.) apart. Pull the stitches quite taut and use an even tension. Work over the roses, leaves and stems. Use two strands of the same thread **a** for the raised stem-stitch, pushing the stitches close together with your fingertip as you form the rows (see page 33).

2. Make the rose buds: Use ribbon **1** and a ribbon or straight stitch to form the small orange buds. Use ribbon **2** and detached chain-stitch for the larger rust coloured buds. A grab stitch at the base of the detached chain-stitch will neaten the shape and a stab stitch with thread **a** or **b** will secure the stitches in place.

3. Make the green stems: Use ribbon **3** and twist it before couching it in place with thread **b**. Space the couching stitches 3 or 4 mm (1/8 in.) apart. Use tiny stab stitches on the edge of the couched stem to re-shape the twisted stem. Add a few thorns alongside the stem in thread **a** or **b** and straight stitch.

4. Make the green calyx on the buds: Use ribbon **3** and ribbon or fly stitch to form the green calyx on the buds.

5. Make the leaves: Use ribbon **3** and ribbon stitch for the smaller leaves and detached chain-stitch for the larger leaves. Use the same ribbon and straight stitch for the thin pointed leaves. Change to thread **b** and use a straight stitch for the very small pointed green leaves. Make a two-wrap French knot for the round green shapes. Use the same thread and straight stitch at the tips of the large green leaves to secure the ribbon stitches in place.

THREAD

a) Gumnut "Stars" pure silk no. 785

b) Chameleon stranded silk no. 61 green

c) Madeira metallic 40 no. 4 gold

Note: use one strand of thread unless suggested otherwise.

RIBBONS

1) Di van Niekerk's 4mm silk no. 51

2) Di van Niekerk's 4mm silk no. 90

3) Di van Niekerk's 4mm silk no. 35

NEEDLES

Crewel size 8 and 9; Chenille size 20; Tapestry size 13 or 16

WHAT ELSE?

- printed or traced design
- backing fabric
- window fabric
- 10 inch (25 cm) hoop

STITCHES USED (SEE STITCH GALLERY PAGES 52-58)

Couching; Detached chain-stitch; Fly stitch; Fly-stitch rose; French knot; Grab stitch; Outline stitch; Raised stem-stitch; Ribbon stitch; Split back-stitch; Stab stitch; Stem stitch; Stem-stitch rose; Straight stitch; Whipped back-stitch: double row; Whipped couching

TO REFRESH YOUR MEMORY

- Before you start *pages 23-28*
- Keeping your work clean and useful hints *page 29*
- Stitches and techniques *pages 31-49*

---

6. Make the roses: Form the centre of the rose in ribbon **1** and a French knot (wrap the ribbon three times around the needle), or use thread **a** and three-wrap French knots, making two or three knots close together. Form the petals in ribbon **2** and make a fly stitch or stem-stitch rose. Use ribbon stitch at the base of the rose to form the open petals.

7. Add more detail: Use thread **b** and straight stitch on the buds to add the green detail. Use thread **a** and gently whip some of the couched stem to add more colour. See whipped couching in the stitch gallery. Change to thread **c** and whip some stems to add golden highlights. Use thread **b** and stem or outline stitch along the edge of the initial. Change to thread **c** and work a short line of stitches along the green edge, here and there, to add golden highlights.

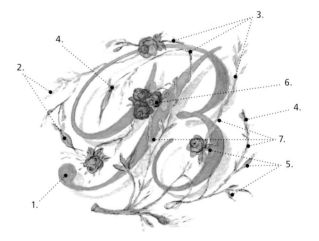

1. Fill in the initial: Use thread **a** and raised stem-stitch to fill in the initial. Use size 24 chenille needle to form the foundation stitches, and a tapestry size 24 for the stem stitch. Keep pushing the stitches close together with your fingernail for a dense texture. See more about raised stem-stitch on page 33.

2. Outline the initial: Use thread **b** and outline the initial in stem or outline stitch to create a shadow and to neaten the edge. Stitch only along one side or on both sides of the initial.

3. Make the thick stems: Use two strands of thread **c** and start at the thick base of the stem at A. Use chain stitch and work upwards, branching off on B stem on the left. Each chain is about 5 mm (³/₁₆ in.) long. End off and start at the base again. Complete stem C in the same way, taking the needle to the back and starting on the other side of the initial. End off at the bud.

Start at the base again, work over the previous rows and complete all the stems in chain stitch. Change to ribbon **1** on a size 24 tapestry needle, start at the base of the stem and use whipped chain-stitch. To form a thick stem, insert the needle under all the rows at the same time. For the thin stems, insert the needle under and over the single row of chain stitch.

4. Make the thin stems: The thin stems are whipped in one or two strands of thread instead of ribbon. Use straight stitch for the finest stems that that branch off from the main stem.

5. Make the large rose leaves: Use ribbon **1** and fly stitch to form the large leaves alongside the roses. Start at the tip with a straight stitch and work down towards the rose in fly stitch. Make two or three fly-stitches close together.

6. Make the large leaves on the stem: Use ribbon **1** and detached chain for the large leaves, work from the stem outwards.

THREAD

a) Chameleon perlé no. 12 cotton no. 39

b) Chameleon stranded silk no. 68

c) Chameleon stranded cotton no. 54

Note: use one strand of thread unless suggested otherwise.

RIBBONS

1) Di van Niekerk's 2mm silk no. 15

2) Di van Niekerk's 4mm silk no. 88

3) Di van Niekerk's 2mm silk no. 74

NEEDLES

Crewel size 8 or 9; Chenille size 20 and 24; Tapestry size 24

WHAT ELSE?

• printed or traced design

• backing fabric

• window fabric

• 10 inch (25 cm) hoop

STITCHES USED (SEE STITCH GALLERY PAGES 52-58)

Chain stitch; Detached chain-stitch; Fly stitch; Fly-stitch rose; French knot; Grab stitch; Outline stitch; Raised stem-stitch; Ribbon stitch; Stem stitch; Straight stitch; Twisted straight-stitch; Whipped chain-stitch

TO REFRESH YOUR MEMORY

• Before you start *pages 23-28*

• Keeping your work clean and useful hints *page 29*

• Stitches and techniques *pages 31-49*

7. **Make the small leaves:** Use ribbon **1** and straight or ribbon stitch for the smaller leaves. Use thread **b** and detached chain or straight stitch for the very small leaves and thorns branching off the stem.

8. **Make the blue rose buds:** Use ribbon **2** on a size 20 chenille needle and make the blue buds along the stem in ribbon or straight stitch. Form the large blue bud (D) in detached chain-stitch. Change to ribbon **3** and use a grab stitch to create a narrow base and add a twisted straight-stitch along the edge of the blue chain stitch for colour.

9. **Make the pink rose buds:** Use ribbon **3** and a two-wrap French knot for the round buds, a ribbon or straight stitch for the straight buds at the tip of the stem and branching off the stems.

10. **Make the roses:** Use ribbon **3** and one or several three-wrap French knots to form the pink centre. Change to ribbon **2** and make a fly-stitch rose around the pink centre. Add a few ribbon stitches at the base of rose E.

11. **Add-ons: detail on tips of the buds and leaves:** Use thread **c** and straight or fly stitch at the tip of the buds and leaves to complete the design.

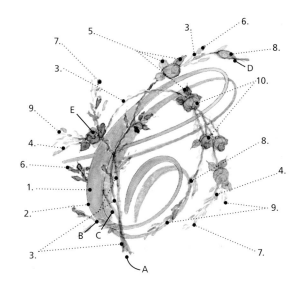

1. **Fill in the initial:** You may like to work off the hoop for this stitch. Use thread **c** and make row after row of chain stitch. The chain stitches are about 3 mm (1/8 in.) in length. See more about chain-stitch filling on page 35. Use a gentle, even tension for a smooth finish.

2. **Outline the initial:** Insert the cloth in the hoop if you have worked the stitch off the hoop. Use thread **a** and stem or outline stitch around the embroidered initial to create a shadow and to neaten the edges.

3. **Make the thick stem:** Use thread **b** and back stitch to form a double row of stitches on the thick stem. The stitches are about 4 mm (1/8 in.) in length. Use ribbon **1** and whip the back stitches, inserting the needle under both rows, to form a thick stem. See page 43.

4. **Make the thin stems:** Use thread **b** and whipped stem or back stitch for the thin stems.

5. **Make the medium size stems:** Use ribbon **1** and twist the ribbon before couching it in place with thread **b**.

Space the couching stitches about 3 mm (1/8 in.) apart and use a gentle tension so as not to flatten the ribbon.

6. **Make the large leaves:** Use ribbon **1** and detached chain-stitch for some leaves, and ribbon stitch for others. Use a straight stitch for long, thin leaves.

7. **Make the small leaves:** Use thread **b** and straight or fly stitch for the very fine leaves at the tip of the buds, and along the stems. Make a two-wrap French knot for the small round leaves.

8. **Make the light orange buds:** Use thread **c** and straight or fly stitch for the tiny buds and two-wrap French knots for the small, round buds. Use ribbon **4** and straight, fly, or ribbon stitch for the larger orange buds.

9. **Make the dark orange buds:** Use ribbon **3** and detached chain-stitch or fly stitch for the large buds. Use ribbon **2** or **4**, add a ribbon stitch in the centre of the bud for an interesting effect. To neaten the base of the large buds, use ribbon **3** and a grab stitch. The long thin

THREAD

a) Chameleon stranded silk no. 66

b) Chameleon stranded cotton no. 6

c) Chameleon stranded cotton no. 50

d) Madeira metallic 40 no. 4 gold

Note: use one strand of thread unless suggested otherwise.

RIBBONS

1) Di van Niekerk's 4mm silk no. 33

2) Di van Niekerk's 4mm silk no. 99

3) Di van Niekerk's 4mm silk no. 90

4) Di van Niekerk's 4mm silk no. 86

NEEDLES

Crewel size 8 and 9; Chenille size 20; Tapestry size 16

WHAT ELSE?

• printed or traced design

• backing fabric

• window fabric

• 10 inch (25 cm) hoop

STITCHES USED (SEE STITCH GALLERY PAGES 52-58)

Back stitch; Chain-stitch filling; Chain stitch; Couching; Detached chain-stitch; Fly stitch; Fly-stitch rose; French knot; Outline stitch; Ribbon stitch; Ribbon-stitch rose; Stem stitch; Stem-stitch rose; Straight stitch; Whipped back-stitch; Whipped back-stitch: double row; Whipped stem-stitch

TO REFRESH YOUR MEMORY

• Before you start *pages 23-28*

• Keeping your work clean and useful hints *page 29*

• Stitches and techniques *pages 31-49*

---

buds branching off the stem are made in straight stitch. Change to thread **a** or **b** and use straight stitch on top of the bud for a realistic finish.

10. Make the golden yellow buds: Use ribbon **2** and straight stitch for the long, thin buds. Use ribbon stitch for the open buds.

11. Make the large roses: Use ribbon **2**, form a yellow centre with a three-wrap French knot. Change to ribbon **3** to make large dark orange fly-stitch or stem-stitch roses. See fly-stitch rose and stem-stitch rose in the stitch gallery. As an alternative, see ribbon-stitch rose in the stitch gallery. Use ribbon **4**, add two or three ribbon stitches on top of the fly stitches to form the lighter petals.

12. Make the small rose: Make the yellow centre with ribbon **2** and a three-wrap French knot. Use ribbon **4** and make a stem-stitch rose. Use a gentle tension for rounded stitches.

13. Embellish the initial: Use thread **d** and whip the stems with the gold thread to add colour. Make two-wrap French knots in the centre of the roses.

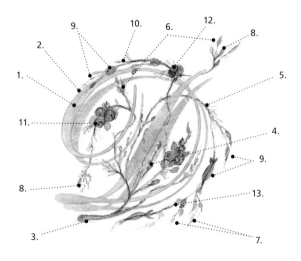

1. Fill in the initial: Use one strand of thread **a**, make rows of chain stitch to fill the initial. See more about chain-stitch filling on page 35. Change to thread **b** and outline the initial in outline, stem or split back-stitch.

2. Make the thick green stems: Use ribbon **1**, form the thick stems by twisting the ribbon and couching it in place with thread **b**. Space couching stitches 3 to 4 mm (¹/₈ in.) apart.

3. Make the fine green stems: Use thread **b** and stem or split back-stitch to form the thin, curved stems leading off the main stems. The straight stems are made in straight or fly stitch.

4. Make the large leaves: Use ribbon **1** and a detached chain-stitch.

5. Make the small leaves: Use ribbon **1** and straight or ribbon stitch. Alternatively, use thread **b** and detached chain-stitch.

6. Make the yellow daisies and buds: Use ribbon **2** and ribbon stitch for the petals and buds. Change to thread **c** and add French knots (three-wraps) in the centre of the yellow daisies.

7. Make the tiny yellow buds: Use thread **c** and

THREAD

	a) Chameleon stranded silk no. 91 Watermelon
	b) Chameleon stranded cotton no. 33 Forest Shade
	c) Chameleon stranded cotton no. 37 Goldrush
	d) Any fine gold metallic thread

Note: use one strand of thread unless suggested otherwise.

RIBBONS

	1) Di van Niekerk's 2mm silk no. 23
	2) Di van Niekerk's 4mm silk no. 53
	3) Di van Niekerk's 7mm silk no. 41
	4) Di van Niekerk's 4mm silk no. 75

NEEDLES

Crewel size 8 or 9; Chenille size mixed pack 18/24; Tapestry size 16

WHAT ELSE?

- printed or traced design
- backing fabric
- window fabric
- 10 inch (25 cm) hoop

STITCHES USED (SEE STITCH GALLERY PAGES 52-58)

Chain-stitch filling; Couching; Detached chain-stitch; Fly stitch; French knot; Loop stitch; Outline stitch; Ribbon stitch; Split back-stitch; Stab stitch; Stem stitch; Straight stitch

TO REFRESH YOUR MEMORY

- Before you start *pages 23-28*
- Keeping your work clean and useful hints *page 29*
- Stitches and techniques *pages 31-49*

---

detached chain or straight stitch for the fine yellow buds branching off the green stems.

8. Make the pink daisies: Use ribbon **3** and ribbon stitch for the daisies. Change to thread **c** and add a few French knots (three wraps) in the centre.

9. Make the pink roses and buds: Use thread **c** to make three-wraps French knots in the centre of the rose. Change to ribbon **3** and make two or three fly stitches to form the rose (see fly-stitch rose in the stitch gallery). Use the same ribbon **3** and straight or ribbon stitch for the pink rose buds.

10. Make the round yellow flowers: Use ribbon **2** and loop stitch for the looped yellow flowers. Work over a size 16 tapestry needle. Leave some loops as they are, or use thread **a** and a three-wrap French knot in the centre of the loop to flatten the stitch.

11. Make the lavender blue flowers: Use ribbon **4** and loop or ribbon stitch for the lavender flowers

12. Optional: embellish the initial: Use gold metallic thread and slanted straight stitches, spaced about 4 mm (1/8 in.) apart. Stitch over the pink initial. To form a - pattern, work back again, crossing over the previous stitches.

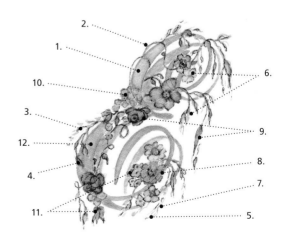

1. **Outline the initial:** Use thread **a** and outline the initial in back stitch. See more about outlining the initial on page 32.

2. **Make the green stems:** Use ribbon **1** and couch the ribbon in place with thread **b**, spacing the stitches 4 mm (¹⁄₈ in.) apart. Where the stem lies behind the initial, take the needle and ribbon to the back and come up on the other side of the initial. Use the same thread and tiny stab stitches to re-shape the ribbon into smooth curves where necessary.

3. **Make the blue stems:** Use thread **c** and stem or outline stitch for the blue stems. The tiny blue stalks at the tip of the stems and leaves are made in straight or fly stitch.

4. **Add colour to the stems:** Use thread **c** and add the blue detail on the stems. Whip the couched green stems, inserting the needle under and over the couched ribbon. Change to thread **d** and add the yellow detail on the green stems in the same way.

5. **Make the leaves:** Use ribbon **2** and detached chain or ribbon stitch for the large leaves, ribbon **1** and detached chain or ribbon stitch for the small leaves. Use thread **b** and the same stitches for the tiny leaves at the tip of the stems and buds.

6. **Make the pink spiderweb roses:** Use thread **a** for the five foundation spokes of the three pink spiderweb roses. Use ribbon **5** to form the spiderweb roses. Make the yellow centre of the rose with ribbon **6** and a two-wrap French knot. Change to thread **d** and make several more three-wrap French knots to complete the centre.

7. **Make the pink buds:** Use ribbon **5** and detached chain-stitch for the large pink buds and ribbon stitch for the smaller buds at the tip of the stems.

8. **Make the pink flowers:** Use ribbon **5** and ribbon stitch for the larger pink petals and a two-wrap French knot for the small pink petals. Use thread **d** and two-wrap French knots in the centre of the flowers.

THREAD

a) Chameleon stranded silk no. 68
b) Chameleon stranded cotton no. 54
c) Chameleon stranded silk no. 19
d) Chameleon stranded silk no. 37

Note: use one strand of thread unless suggested otherwise.

RIBBONS

1) Di van Niekerk's 2mm silk no. 16
2) Di van Niekerk's 4mm silk no. 32
3) Di van Niekerk's 4mm silk no. 89
4) Di van Niekerk's 4mm silk no. 81
5) Di van Niekerk's 4mm silk no. 42
6) Di van Niekerk's 4mm silk no. 55

NEEDLES

Crewel size 9 or 10; Chenille size 20 and 22; Tapestry size 13

WHAT ELSE?

• printed or traced design
• backing fabric
• window fabric
• 10 inch (25 cm) hoop

STITCHES USED (SEE STITCH GALLERY PAGES 52-58)

Back stitch; Couching; Detached chain-stitch; Fly stitch; Loop stitch; Outline stitch; Ribbon stitch; Spiderweb rose; Stab stitch; Stem stitch; Straight stitch; Whipped couching

TO REFRESH YOUR MEMORY

• Before you start *pages 23-28*
• Keeping your work clean and useful hints *page 29*
• Stitches and techniques *pages 31-49*

9. Make the lavender blue flowers: Use ribbon **4** and, working over a spare tapestry needle, form a loop stitch for each flower. Use thread **c** and add one French knot on top of each loop, wrapping the thread twice around the needle.

10. Make the royal blue flowers: Use ribbon **3** and, working over a spare tapestry needle, form a loop stitch for each flower. Use thread **c** and add one French knot on top of each loop, wrapping the thread twice around the needle. See step 12 to add the golden highlights.

11. Make the yellow daisies: Use ribbon **6** and detached chain-stitch for some petals, and ribbon stitch for others. Work from the centre outwards. Use thread **d**, make a two-wrap French knot at the tip of each petal and fill the centre of the flower with the same stitch.

12. Add-on: add golden highlights: Use thread **d** and straight stitch at the tip of and between the leaves to add more colour. Use a grab stitch at the base of the

large buds to form a narrow base and to add colour at the same time. Add a few two-wrap French knots between the blue flowers.

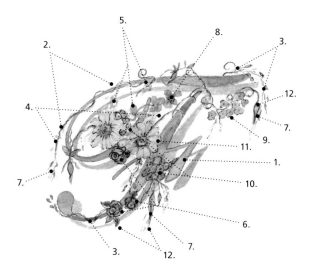

1. Fill in the initial: Use thread **a** and fill in the initial with rows of stem stitch. Make the rows close together for a smooth finish. Fill in any gaps with straight stitch. See more about stem-stitch filling on page 32.

2. Outline the initial: Use thread **b** and stem or outline stitch to create a dark pink shadow along the bottom edge of the initial. Change to thread **c** and make a second row of lilac stitches alongside the dark pink row. Proceed along the edge of the initial so that the entire initial is outlined.

3. Make the thick stem of the pink cosmos: Use two strands of thread **d**, start on the thick base at A. Make two chain stitches, take the needle to the back. Start on the other side of the initial, proceed up the stem and end off at the pink flower. Use ribbon **1** to whip the chain stitches (see whipped chain-stitch on page 58).

4. Make all the other stems: Use ribbon **1** and couch it in place with thread **d**. Twist the ribbon as you couch it in place. For invisible stitching, use tiny stab stitches instead of couching stitches to secure the twisted ribbon in place and to re-shape the stem where necessary.

5. Make the leaves: Use ribbon **1** for all the leaves. The large leaves of the cosmos flower are made in fly stitch, the rose leaves in ribbon or straight stitch and the leaves of the berries with detached chain-stitch.

6. Make the berries: Use thread **c** on a size 10 crewel or straw size 9 needle and attach the beads to form the berries. For the small berries at B, use thread **c** and two-wrap French knots.

7. Make the lilac roses: Make spiderweb roses. Use thread **c** for the five foundation spokes and ribbon **3 to** make the two lilac spiderweb roses. Change to thread **e**

THREAD

	a) Chameleon stranded silk: protea no. 3
	b) Chameleon stranded silk: protea no. 5
	c) Chameleon stranded cotton no. 95
	d) DMC stranded cotton no. 3348
	e) DMC stranded cotton no. 3078

Note: use one strand of thread unless suggested otherwise.

RIBBONS

	1) Di van Niekerk's 4mm silk no. 118
	2) Di van Niekerk's 7mm silk no. 127
	3) Di van Niekerk's 4mm silk no. 73
	4) Di van Niekerk's 7mm silk no. 108

NEEDLES

Crewel size 9; Chenille size 18 and 20; Tapestry size 13 or 16; Crewel size 10 or straw size 9 for beading

WHAT ELSE?

- printed or traced design
- backing fabric
- window fabric
- 10 inch (25 cm) hoop
- small seed beads: lavender/lilac

STITCHES USED (SEE STITCH GALLERY PAGES 52-58)

Chain stitch; Couching; Detached chain-stitch; Fly stitch; French knot; Loop stitch; Outline stitch; Ribbon stitch; Ribbon stitch with curled-up tips; Spiderweb rose; Stab stitch; Stem-stitch filling; Stem stitch; Straight stitch; Whipped chain-stitch

TO REFRESH YOUR MEMORY

- Before you start *pages 23-28*
- Keeping your work clean and useful hints *page 29*
- Stitches and techniques *pages 31-49*
- Attaching a bead *page 38*

---

and add three French knots in the centre of each rose. Wrap thread three times around the needle.

8. Make the small pink flowers: Use ribbon **2** and form a loop stitch for each flower working over a spare tapestry needle. Use thread **c** and add two French knots on top of each loop; wrap the thread twice around the needle.

9. Make the large pink dog roses: Use ribbon **2** and ribbon stitch with curled-up tips for each petal. Use thread **b** to make dark pink French knots in the centre, and thread **e** to make the yellow knots. Wrap the thread twice around the needle.

10. Make the large pink cosmos: Use ribbon **4** and ribbon stitch with curled-up tips for each petal. Use thread **c** and two-wrap French knots to form the lilac shadow in the centre of the flower. Change to thread **e** and use the same stitch to complete the yellow centre.

11. Add-ons: add the dark pink detail: Use thread **b** and straight stitch between and on top of some of the leaves to add colour.

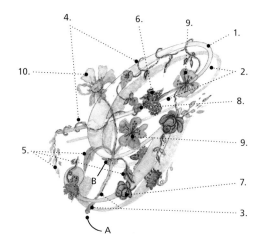

1. Fill in the initial: Use thread **a** and make rows of chain stitch alongside each other to fill in the turquoise initial. Make short chains, about 2 mm ($^1/_{16}$ in.), with some even shorter to accommodate the curves.

2. Make the stems: Use ribbon **1** and twist it before couching it in place with thread **b**. Use a gentle tension so as not to flatten the ribbon. Make the thin stems in thread **b** and whipped back-stitch.

3. Make the leaves: Use ribbon **1** and straight or ribbon stitch to form the green leaves on the stem, working from the stem outwards. Use ribbon **2** and do the same for the turquoise leaves. Change to ribbon **1** and use several fly stitches in a row to form the large leaves of the dog roses and the pink daisy. Change to thread **b** and use detached chain, fly or straight stitch for the tiny green leaves, then use thread **c** and do the same for the tiny pink leaves.

4. Make the dark pink roses: Use ribbon **3** and make the three dark pink roses with a ribbon-stitch rose. Start with thread **d** and make five or six French knots (three wraps) to form the centre of the rose. Change to ribbon **3** and form the petals with ribbon stitch. Work over a spare tapestry needle to form loose, raised petals and use the tapestry needle to re-shape the petals to form an attractive rose.

5. Make the purple wisteria: Use thread **c** and French knots to form the lilac flowers, wrapping the thread three or four times around the needle. Refer to the photograph above as a guide. To add more colour, use the same thread **c** and whip the couched green stems.

6. Make the pink dog roses: Use ribbon **4** and ribbon stitch with curled-up tips to form the turned up petals. Use ribbon stitch for the smaller petals, working from the centre outwards. Use thread **d** and three-wrap

THREAD

	a) Gumnut "Stars" pure silk no. 405
	b) Chameleon stranded silk no. 40
	c) Chameleon stranded silk no. 38
	d) Chameleon stranded silk no. 37

Note: use one strand of thread unless suggested otherwise.

RIBBONS

	1) Di van Niekerk's 4mm silk no. 30
	2) Di van Niekerk's 2mm silk no. 69
	3) Di van Niekerk's 4mm silk no. 41
	4) Di van Niekerk's 7mm silk no. 43
	5) Di van Niekerk's 7mm silk no. 52

NEEDLES

Crewel size 9 or 10; Chenille size 18, 20 and 22;
Tapestry size 13 or 16

WHAT ELSE?

- printed or traced design
- backing fabric
- window fabric
- 10 inch (25 cm) hoop

STITCHES USED (SEE STITCH GALLERY PAGES 52-58)

Chain stitch; Couching; Detached chain-stitch; Fly stitch; French knot; Loop stitch; Ribbon stitch; Ribbon-stitch rose; Ribbon stitch with curled-up tips; Split back-stitch; Stab stitch; Stem stitch; Straight stitch; Whipped back-stitch

TO REFRESH YOUR MEMORY

- Before you start *pages 23-28*
- Keeping your work clean and useful hints *page 29*
- Stitches and techniques *pages 31-49*

French knots to form the yellow stamens in the centre of the rose. Use the same thread and tiny stab stitches to re-shape and secure the tips of the petals.

7. Make the yellow flowers: Use ribbon **5** and, working over the spare tapestry needle, form a loop stitch for each yellow flower. Use thread **c** or **d** and make a three-wrap French knot in the centre of the loop.

8. Embellish the initial: Use thread **c** and stem or split back-stitch along one edge of the initial to form a dark shadow and to add colour at the same time.

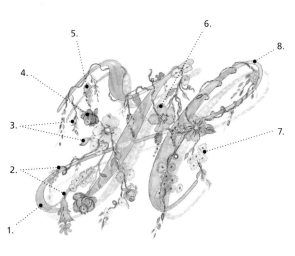

1. **Fill in the initial:** Use one or two strands of thread **a** and fill in the initial in raised stem-stitch. See more about raised stem-stitch on page 33. Change to one strand of thread **b** and outline the edge of the initial in outline or stem stitch.

2. **Form the stems:** Use one strand of thread **b** and split, back or stem stitch.

3. **Make the decorative curls:** Use ribbon **1** and fly stitch to form the curls. Add a small bead in the centre of each stitch.

4. **Make the small leaves:** Use ribbon **1** and ribbon stitch for the small leaves.

5. **Make the forget-me-not flower:** Use ribbon **2** and French knots, wrapping the ribbon twice around the needle. Change to ribbon **3** and use the same stitch for the yellow centre.

6. **Make the large leaves:** Use ribbon **4** and detached chain-stitch for the large leaves.

THREAD

a) Chameleon stranded cotton no. 29

b) Chameleon stranded cotton no. 33

c) DMC precious metal effects no. E168

Note: use one strand of thread unless suggested otherwise.

RIBBONS

1) Di van Niekerk's 2mm silk no. 16

2) Di van Niekerk's 2mm silk no. 68

3) Di van Niekerk's 2mm silk no. 55

4) Di van Niekerk's 4mm silk no. 16

5) Di van Niekerk's 4mm silk no. 68

NEEDLES

Crewel size 8 or 9; Chenille size 20 and 22; Crewel size 10 or straw size 9 for beading; Tapestry size 13 or 16

WHAT ELSE?

- printed or traced design
- backing fabric
- window fabric
- 10 inch (25 cm) hoop
- 12 small glass seed beads: turquoise or green

STITCHES USED (SEE STITCH GALLERY PAGES 52-58)

Detached chain; Fly stitch; French knot; Outline stitch; Raised stem-stitch; Ribbon stitch; Split back-stitch; Stab stitch; Stem stitch; Straight stitch; Whipped back-stitch; Whipped stem-stitch

TO REFRESH YOUR MEMORY

- Before you start *pages 23-28*
- Keeping your work clean and useful hints *page 29*
- Stitches and techniques *pages 31-49*
- Attaching a bead *page 38*

7. Make the blue petals: Use ribbon **5** and form the petals behind the front petals in straight stitch. Make the front petals in ribbon stitch. Use thread **b** and tiny stab stitches to secure the petals at the tip and base.

8. Add-ons: make the silver highlights: Use thread **c** and work slanted straight stitches over the raised initial. Whip the stems with the same thread (see whipped stem and whipped back-stitch on page 58).

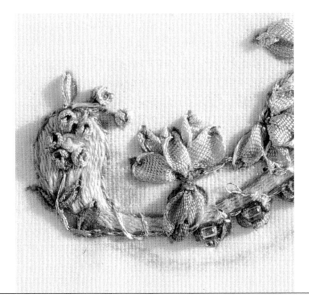

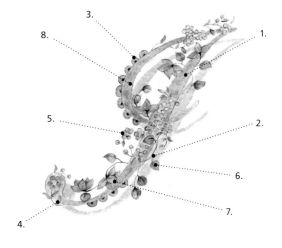

1. **Fill in the initial:** Use one or two strands of thread **a** and fill in the blue part with rows of stem stitch (see stem-stitch filling on page 32). Work over the flowers and black lines, these will be added on top later. Fill in the gaps in straight stitch. Change to thread **b** and use the same stitch for the pale green sections on the initial, then use thread **c** for the stone-coloured patches on the initial. Refer to the colour picture as a guide.

2. **Outline the initial:** Use thread **d** and outline the edges of the initial in stem or split stitch to create a shadow and to neaten the edges.

3. **Form the zigzag pattern:** Use thread **e** and slanted straight stitches to form the zigzag pattern on the initial. Refer to the colour photograph as a guide. Work on top of the stitches and insert the needle precisely on the edge of the initial for a neat finish.

4. **Make the dots:** Use thread **e** and the crewel size 10, or straw size 9 needle and add three black beads on the

top part of the initial near A. Change to thread **a** and form the remaining dots on the initial with two-wrap French knots.

5. **Make the pale green stems:** Use ribbon **1** and couch it in place with thread **a** to form the twirled stems. Or choose blanket stitch and use a very loose tension as you form each stitch around the initial. Start at the top of the initial at A and work over the curve of the initial to the flower at B. Start at C and end off at the flower. Start at D, end off at E, start at F, end off at the flower. Use thread **b** and tiny stab stitches to re-shape the stem where necessary.

6. **Make the pale blue stems:** Use ribbon **2** and form the curled stems above the flower (near C) by couching the ribbon in place with thread **b**. Use ribbon **1** and whip the couched ribbon to add the green colour. Repeat for the stems trailing off the initial near D and F.

7. **Make the flowers:** Use ribbon **1** and detached chain-

THREAD

a) Gumnut Aztecs pure silk: turquoise light

b) Chameleon stranded silk: Knysna Forest 1

c) Chameleon stranded silk no. 85

d) Chameleon stranded silk no. 68

e) DMC stranded cotton no. 844

Note: use one strand of thread unless suggested otherwise.

RIBBONS

1) Di van Niekerk's 2mm silk no. 18

2) Di van Niekerk's 2mm silk no. 129

NEEDLES

Crewel size 8 or 9; Chenille size 22; Tapestry size 20;
Crewel size 10 or straw size 9 for beading

WHAT ELSE?

- printed or traced design
- window fabric
- small seed beads: black
- backing fabric
- 10 inch (25 cm) hoop

STITCHES USED (SEE STITCH GALLERY PAGES 52-58)

Blanket stitch; Couching; Detached chain-stitch; Fly stitch;
French knot; Grab stitch; Ribbon stitch; Split stitch; Stab stitch;
Stem-stitch filling; Stem stitch; Straight stitch; Whipped couching

TO REFRESH YOUR MEMORY

- Before you start *pages 23-28*
- Keeping your work clean and useful hints *page 29*
- Stitches and techniques *pages 31-49*
- Attaching a bead *page 38*

---

stitch to form the green petals of the seven flowers. Work from the centre outwards. Use thread **e** and make one or two French knots in the centre of each flower. Wrap the thread twice around the needle. To soften the effect, you could add another French knot on top using thread **a**.

8. Make the green leaves: Use ribbon **1** and ribbon or detached chain-stitch to form the small green leaves along the stem. Use thread **a** and stab stitch at the tip of the ribbon stitch to secure it and to add more colour.

9. Make the blue buds: Use ribbon **2** and detached chain-stitch for the blue buds; work from the stem outwards. Make the small blue leaves in ribbon stitch. Use thread **a** and a stab stitch at the tip of each ribbon stitch. Make two-wrap French knots for the tiny round buds.

10. Make the green calyx around the buds: Use ribbon **1** and a fly or grab stitch around the base of the blue buds. Insert the needle further away to create a long thin stem.

11. Add-ons: brown stems and shadows: Use thread **e** and straight stitch to form the dark brown stems at A and a short line of back stitch on the edges of the initial to form patches of dark shadows here and there.

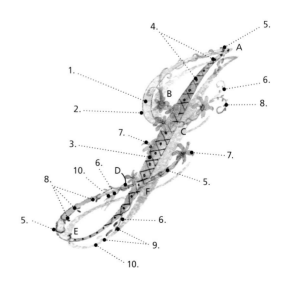

1. Fill in the initial: Use thread **a**, and rows of stem stitch to fill in the initial. See more about stem-stitch filling on page 32. Work over the flowers, which will be added on top later. Use a small stab stitch to re-shape the stitches on the rounded curves. Fill in the gaps with straight stitch for a smooth texture. Use thread **d** and stem or outline stitch along the edge of the initial to create a shadow and to neaten the edge.

2. Make the stems: Use thread **b** and form the green stems in back stitch about 4 mm (¹/₈ in.) long. Change to ribbon **1** and whip each back stitch to form a raised life-like stem. Use a gentle tension as you wrap the ribbon under and over each stitch.

3. Make the green leaves: Use ribbon **1 and** make the large leaves of the berries. Start at the tip with a straight stitch and continue with rows of fly stitch. The remaining leaves on the stem are made in detached chain, ribbon or straight stitch. Change to thread **b** and make the

tiny straight leaves at the tips of the stems in straight or fly stitch.

4. Make the pink leaves: Use ribbon **3** and ribbon stitch for the pink leaves. To form a larger, raised stitch make another ribbon stitch on top of the first (padded ribbon-stitch). Use thread **a** and a detached chain-stitch or French knot on top of the pink leaves. Change to thread **c** and make the small pink, straight leaves in straight stitch. Use two-wrap French knots for the tiny round dots at the tip of the stems.

5. Make the blue leaves and stem: Use ribbon **2** and ribbon stitch to form the blue leaves on the initial, roses and stems. Use thread **a** and straight stitch at the tip of each leaf, and the stems. The tiny round blue dots are made with a two-wrap French knot; the thin blue stem is made in stem stitch.

6. Make the berries: Use ribbon **4** and one-wrap French knots to form the berries.

THREAD

	a) Chameleon stranded silk: two oceans no. 3
	b) Chameleon stranded cotton no. 32
	c) Chameleon stranded silk: protea no. 2
	d) Chameleon stranded silk no. 68
	c) DMC precious metal effects no. E168

Note: use one strand of thread unless suggested otherwise.

RIBBONS

	1) Di van Niekerk's 2mm silk no. 28
	2) Di van Niekerk's 4mm silk no. 67
	3) Di van Niekerk's 4mm silk no. 40
	4) Di van Niekerk's 2mm silk no. 73
	5) Di van Niekerk's 4mm silk no. 56

NEEDLES

Crewel size 9 or 10; Chenille size 20 and 22; Tapestry size 13

WHAT ELSE?

- printed or traced design
- backing fabric
- window fabric
- 10 inch (25 cm) hoop

STITCHES USED (SEE STITCH GALLERY PAGES 52-58)

Back stitch; Detached chain-stitch; Fly- and ribbon-stitch rose; Fly stitch; Fly-stitch rose; French knot; Padded ribbon-stitch; Ribbon stitch; Ribbon stitch with curled-up tips; Stem-stitch filling; Straight stitch; Whipped back-stitch

TO REFRESH YOUR MEMORY

- Before you start *pages 23-28*
- Keeping your work clean and useful hints *page 29*
- Stitches and techniques *pages 31-49*

---

7. Make the pink roses: Use two strands of thread **c** and make a three-wrap French knot to form the pink centre of the rose. Use ribbon **3** and make two or three fly stitches (see fly-stitch rose and fly- and ribbon-stitch rose on page 54). Add one or two ribbon stitches at the base of the rose to form the open petals. Use thread **c** again, add more French knots in the centre, if necessary.

8. Make the pink dog roses: Use ribbon **4** and ribbon stitch with curled-up tips to form the pink petals. Work from the centre outwards. Use thread **c** and a three-wrap French knot in the centre of the rose.

9. Make the yellow flowers: Use ribbon **5** and, working over a spare tapestry needle, form a loop stitch for each flower. Use thread **c** and add a two-wrap French knot on top of each loop.

10. Add-ons: silver highlights: Use thread **e** and straight stitch to highlight the veins on the large leaves.

Whip the stems with the silver thread, inserting the needle under and over the stitches with a gentle tension so as not to flatten the stem. Add silver highlights in straight stitch on some ribbon leaves, or wherever else you would like to add highlights.

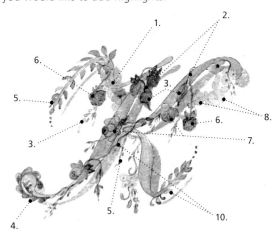

1. **Fill in the initial:** Use thread **a** to couch thread **b**, filling in the initial. Make the rows of couching close together, which will form the foundation stitch for the satin couching. (See satin couching on page 35.) Work over the flowers and stems as these will be made on top later. Use thread **a** and work satin stitch over the couching. Make the stitches close together, using a gentle and even tension for a neat finish.

2. **Outline the initial:** Use thread **c** and make a row of chain stitch on one edge of the initial to create an interesting shadow and to neaten the edges of the pink stitches. Change to thread **e** and form a row of stem stitch along the opposite edge of the initial.

3. **Make the green stems:** Use thread **d** and back stitch to form the green stems. Make back stitches about 3 mm (⅛ in.) in length. Change to ribbon **1** and whip the back stitches to form the thick stems. The very fine stems are whipped with thread **d**.

4. **Make the leaves:** Use thread **d** and make the leaves at A and D in fly stitch. Use a straight stitch for the tiny leaves at the end of the stems. Change to ribbon **1** and make the small leaves at B and C in detached chain-stitch. The last leaf at the end is a one-wrap French knot. Use a detached chain for the larger leaves below the blue flower and between the yellow flowers.

5. **Embellish the leaves:** Change to thread **c** and use feather stitch on top of the leaves at B and C. Work from the tip of the leaves towards the initial. Use thread **c** and fly stitch on top of the large leaf at D, and use thread **a** and straight stitch to make the pink veins on the small leaves at A.

6. **Make the pink and yellow buds:** Use ribbon **2** and **3** and a detached chain or ribbon stitch for the larger buds and straight stitch for the tiny buds.

7. **Make the calyx of the buds:** Use ribbon **1** and form the green calyx at the base of the buds in fly or grab stitch.

THREAD

~~	a) Chameleon stranded silk no. 91
~~	b) Chameleon perlé (no. 8) thread no. 91
~~	c) Chameleon stranded silk no. 12
~~	d) Chameleon stranded silk no. 40
~~	e) DMC precious metal effects no. E168

Note: use one strand of thread unless suggested otherwise.

RIBBONS

~~	1) Di van Niekerk's 2mm silk no. 16
~~	2) Di van Niekerk's 4mm no. 94
~~	3) Di van Niekerk's 4mm silk no. 55
~~	4) Di van Niekerk's 4mm silk no. 40
~~	5) Di van Niekerk's 7mm silk no. 64

WHAT ELSE?

- printed or traced design
- window fabric
- tiny seed beads: blue and pink
- backing fabric
- 10 inch (25 cm) hoop

NEEDLES

Crewel size 7 for metallic thread; Crewel size 8 or 9 for silk threads; Crewel size 10 or straw size 9 for beading; Chenille mixed pack size 18/24; Tapestry size 13 or 16; Straw size 3 or crewel size 5 for perlé thread

STITCHES USED (SEE STITCH GALLERY PAGES 52-58)

Back stitch; Chain stitch; Detached chain-stitch; Feather stitch; Fly stitch; French knot; Grab stitch; Loop stitch; Loose/puffed ribbon stitch; Ribbon stitch; Satin couching; Stab stitch; Stem stitch; Straight stitch; Whipped back-stitch

TO REFRESH YOUR MEMORY

- Before you start *pages 23-28*
- Keeping your work clean and useful hints *page 29*
- Stitches and techniques *pages 31-49*
- Attaching a bead *page 38*

---

8. **Make the clusters of pink flowers:** Use ribbon **2** for the light pink petals and ribbon **4** for the darker pink petals. Form each petal in ribbon stitch working over a spare tapestry needle to form loose/puffed ribbon stitches. Work from the centre outwards, overlapping some petals for a dense texture. Add a pink bead in the centre of each flower. Use ribbon **1** and loose/puffed ribbon stitches to form the green leaves between the pink flowers.

9. **Make the yellow flowers:** Use ribbon **4** and loosely wrapped French knots (three-wraps) for the large yellow flowers near C and D. Use a loop stitch for the smaller flowers near A. Change to thread **a** or **d** and add a three-wrap French knot in the centre of each flower.

10. **Make the blue flowers:** Use ribbon **5** and make the large blue petals in loop stitch, the smaller petals in ribbon stitch. Use thread **c** and tiny stab stitches in the centre of the flower to secure the loops. Add a blue bead in the centre of the flower.

11. **Add-ons: add the silver and pink highlights:** Using thread **e** or **a**, whip the stems with the silver or pink thread to add the highlights. Use thread **e** and make a straight stitch on top of and between the leaves.

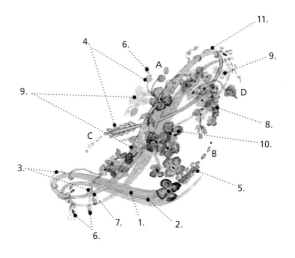

1. Fill in the initial: Thread a size 7 of 8 crewel needle with one strand of thread **a** (normal length). Cut another 70 cm (28 in.) length of the same thread but don't separate the strands as this is the laid thread. Thread on a size 22 chenille needle and start in the centre of the shape at A. Couch the laid thread in place every 3 to 4 mm (⅛ in.) Twirl the thread to fill the shape as shown in the photograph. Fill the initial with row after row of couching, working up to the sharp point at B. Work down to the curve at C, up to D and end off at E. End off and start with a fresh thread when necessary (see couching on page 34).

2. Outline the initial: Use one strand of thread **c** and back or stem stitch to outline the initial for a neat edge and to create a golden shadow.

3. Make the stems: Use two strands of thread **b** and backstitch to form the all the stems in the design. Make the stitches about 3 mm (⅛ in.) long. Use ribbon **1** and whip the back stitches with the ribbon to form the rounded green stems. Use thread **b** to whip the narrow blue stems. Use thread **c** and stem stitch to form the twirled golden stems leading off the green stems. Whip the green stem with the same golden thread to add colour, or use back or stem stitch alongside the green stem.

4. Make the green leaves: Use ribbon **1** and detached chain-stitch for the larger green leaves. Use ribbon or straight stitch for the smaller green leaves. Work from the stem outwards. Use thread **c** and straight stitch at the tip of some leaves to add colour.

5. Make the green filigree shapes: Use ribbon **1** and fly or detached chain-stitch to form the green filigree shapes at A and E. Change to thread **c** and add a straight stitch down the centre of each shape. Use the same thread on a size 10 crewel or size 9 straw needle and attach an orange bead between the shapes.

6. Make the blue buds and leaves: Use ribbon **2** and

THREAD

a) Chameleon stranded rayon no. 31

b) Gumnut Aztecs pure silk: turquoise dark

c) Chameleon stranded silk no. 37

Note: use one strand of thread unless suggested otherwise.

RIBBONS

1) Di van Niekerk's 2mm silk no. 27

2) Di van Niekerk's 2mm silk no. 69

3) Di van Niekerk's 4mm silk no. 99

4) Di van Niekerk's 4mm silk no. 90

NEEDLES

Crewel size 8 or 9; Chenille size 20 and 22;

Tapestry size 22 or 24; Crewel size 10 or straw size 9 for beading

WHAT ELSE?

- printed or traced design
- backing fabric
- window fabric
- 10 inch (25 cm) hoop
- small glass seed beads: burnt orange

STITCHES USED (SEE STITCH GALLERY PAGES 52-58)

Back stitch; Couching; Detached chain-stitch; Fly- and ribbon-stitch rose; Fly stitch; Fly-stitch rose; French knot; Ribbon stitch; Stem stitch; Straight stitch; Whipped back-stitch

TO REFRESH YOUR MEMORY

- Before you start *pages 23-28*
- Keeping your work clean and useful hints *page 29*
- Stitches and techniques *pages 31-49*
- Attaching a bead *page 38*

---

a detached chain or ribbon stitch to form the blue buds and leaves. Use thread **c** and straight stitch on the tip of some shapes to secure the stitch and to add colour.

7. Make the golden yellow buds and leaves: Use ribbon **3** and ribbon stitch to form the golden buds and leaves. Use 1 strand of thread **a** and make a French knot (one wrap) or straight stitch to add a touch of colour alongside the golden leaves.

8. Make the yellow rose: Use thread **1** and make a three-wrap French knot to form the orange centre. Use ribbon **3** and make a fly-stitch rose. Make two or three fly stitches and add two or three ribbon stitches on top to form the open petals at the base of the rose.

9. Make the orange roses and buds: Use ribbon **4** and make the orange roses as you did the yellow rose above. The orange bud at C is made in detached chain-stitch. Use a long anchoring stitch as you take the ribbon to the back. Change to thread **b** and make two or

three straight stitches at the tip of the bud. Use a grab stitch at the base of the bud to neaten the shape.

10. Add-ons: blue and orange detail: Use thread **b** and a three-wrap French knot to make the blue dots on the initial. Use a gentle tension so that the knot sits on top of the orange stitches. Make a straight stitch to form the tiny blue stalks at the end of the stems. Attach an orange bead to form the orange dots in the design.

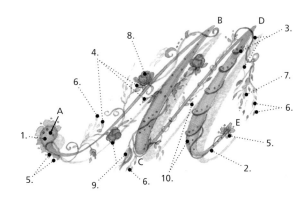

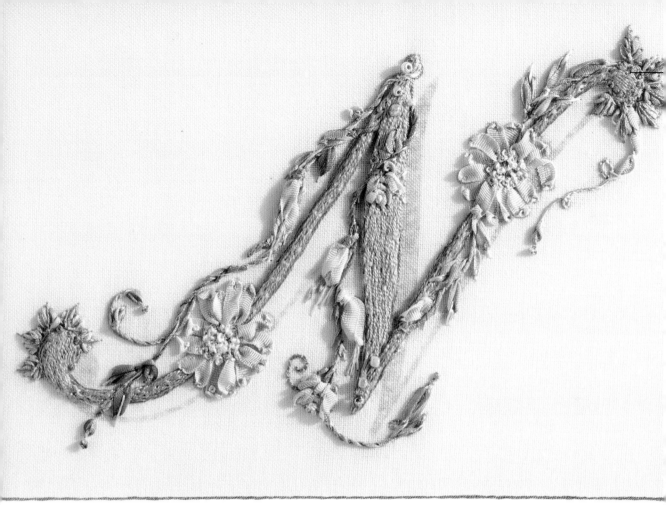

1. **Fill in the initial:** Use two strands of thread **a** and form the foundation stitches for raised stem-stitch. Work horizontal stitches from side to side spaced about 3 mm (¹/₈ in.) apart. Pull the stitches quite taut and use an even tension. Work over the flowers, leaves and stems. Use two strands of the same thread **a** for the raised stem-stitch, pushing the stitches close together with your fingertip as you form the subsequent rows (see page 33).

2. **Make the turquoise blue stems:** Use two strands of thread **b** and form the turquoise blue stems in back stitch. Refer to the design for the position of the stems, making stitches about 3 mm (¹/₈ in.) in length. Use a gentle, even tension and make shorter stitches when you reach a curve. Use ribbon **2** and whip the back stitches to form the thick blue stems. For very fine stems it is not necessary to whip the back stitches.

3. **Make the light green stems:** Use two strands of thread **b** and form the green stems in back stitch as you did above. To form the thick green stems, use ribbon **1** and whip the

back stitches as you did before. To form the thin green stems, use thread **c** and whip the back stitches as you did before.

4. **Make the light green leaves:** Use ribbon **1** and detached chain-stitch to form the light green leaves, working from the stem outwards. Add a two-wrap French knot at the end of the light green stems. Change to thread **d** and make a straight stitch at the tip of some leaves for an interesting play with colour.

5. **Make the leaves on the rounded ends:** Use ribbon **1** and start at the sharp tip of the leaf with a straight stitch. Make two or three fly stitches close together to fill in the shape of a leaf. Change to thread **b** and add a straight stitch down the centre of the leaf. Change to thread **e** and add a second straight stitch alongside to create interesting highlights.

6. **Make the turquoise blue leaves:** Use ribbon **2** and detached chain-stitch to form the turquoise blue leaves on the stem. Work from the stem outwards. Add a one-wrap French knot at the end of the blue stems. Change to thread **c** and add a light green straight stitch on some leaves. Use thread **b**

THREAD

 a) Gumnut Aztecs turquoise (medium)

b) Gumnut Aztecs turquoise (dark)

c) Chameleon stranded silk no. 40

d) Chameleon stranded silk no. 23

e) Kreinik blending filament no. 032 pearl

Note: use one strand of thread unless suggested otherwise.

RIBBONS

1) Di van Niekerk's 2mm silk ribbon no. 30

2) Di van Niekerk's 2mm silk ribbon no. 69

3) Di van Niekerk's 4mm silk ribbon no. 127

NEEDLES

Crewel size 8 or 9; Chenille size 20 and 22; Tapestry size 24;
Crewel size 10 or straw size 9 for beading

WHAT ELSE?

• printed or traced design
• window fabric
• small seed beads: lilac/baby pink
• backing fabric
• 10 inch (25 cm) hoop

STITCHES USED (SEE STITCH GALLERY PAGES 52-58)

Back stitch; Detached chain-stitch; Fly stitch; Fly-stitch rose;
French knot; Outline stitch; Raised stem-stitch; Ribbon stitch;
Stab stitch; Stem stitch; Straight stitch; Twisted ribbon-stitch;
Whipped back-stitch

TO REFRESH YOUR MEMORY

• Before you start *pages 23-28*
• Keeping your work clean and useful hints *page 29*
• Stitches and techniques *pages 31-49*
• Attaching a bead *page 38*

---

to add the dark turquoise stitches at the tip of the leaves.

7. Make the pink buds: Use ribbon **3** and ribbon or straight stitch to form the tiny pink buds. Use detached chain-stitch for the large teardrop shape buds. Make a ribbon stitch on top if you need to form a fuller bud. Use thread **c** or **d,** add a few straight stitches at the tip of the buds. To neaten the detached chain-stitches, use thread **d** or **b** and a grab stitch. To form the green calyx on the side of the large bud, use ribbon **1** and a fly stitch. Change to thread **d** and use tiny stab stitches to re-shape the calyx if necessary.

8. Make the pink roses: Use thread **d** and make four or five French knots in the centre of the rose. Wrap the thread twice around the needle. Change to ribbon **3** and make fly-stitch roses. Use a gentle tension for a soft, open rose.

9. Make the pink daisies: Use ribbon **3** and ribbon stitch to form the pink daisies. Use twisted ribbon-stitch for the curved petals. Work from the centre outwards. Change to thread **d** and make two-wrap French knots in the centre of the daisy. Add a yellow knot at the tip of some daisy petals.

Use thread **c** and the same stitch to make the green knots in the centre.

10. Embellish the initial: Use thread **b** and stem or outline stitch along the edges of the initial to create a shadow and to neaten the edge. Add three-wrap French knots on the rounded ends of the initial. Change to thread **e** and whip some stems again with the shiny thread to add interesting highlights. Attach three pink beads at the sharp points of the initial.

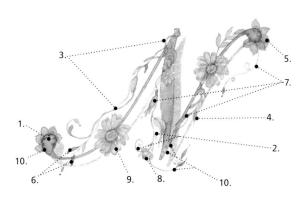

1. Fill in the initial: Use thread **a** and fill in the orange part of the initial with rows of stem stitch. Make the rows close together for a smooth finish. (See stem-stitch filling on page 32.) Change to thread **b** and do the same for the lilac section on the initial. Use thread **c** and stem stitch to create the dark line between the orange and lilac sections. Use straight or back stitches to create the zigzag pattern on the lilac section.

2. Make the stems: Use thread **d** and stem stitch or split back-stitch to create the twirled green stems of

the lilac flowers. Use two or three rows of stem stitch made close together for the upright stems of the tulips and whip the stitches with the same thread to create a smooth, rounded stem.

3. Make the lilac flowers: Use ribbon **1** and straight stitch, working over a spare tapestry needle for the dark lilac petals. Use ribbon **2** and the same stitch for the pink petals. Change to thread **e** and make a straight stitch at the base of each stitch to secure it in place.

4. Make the leaves: Use ribbon **3** and twisted straight-stitch to form the large leaves, use ribbon or straight stitch for the smaller leave. Use thread **d** and tiny stab stitches to re-shape and secure the leaves. For the rose leaves, use ribbon **4** and fly stitch. Start with a straight stitch at the tip and make two or three fly stitches close

THREAD

	a) Gumnut "Stars" pure silk no. 784
	b) Chameleon stranded silk no. 90
	c) Chameleon stranded silk or cotton no. 8
	d) Gumnut "Stars" pure silk no. 607
	e) Chameleon stranded silk protea no. 2
	f) Any fine silver metallic thread

Note: use one strand of thread unless suggested otherwise.

RIBBONS

	1) Di van Niekerk's 2mm silk no. 76
	2) Di van Niekerk's 2mm silk no. 43
	3) Di van Niekerk's 7mm silk no. 132
	4) Di van Niekerk's 2mm silk no. 19
	5) Di van Niekerk's 7mm silk no. 41
	6) Di van Niekerk's 7mm silk no. 127

NEEDLES

Crewel size 9 or 10; Chenille size 18, 20 and 22;
Tapestry size 13 or 16

WHAT ELSE?

- printed or traced design
- backing fabric
- window fabric
- 10 inch (25 cm) hoop

STITCHES USED (SEE STITCH GALLERY PAGES 52-58)

Back stitch; Fly stitch; French knot; Ribbon stitch; Ribbon-stitch rose; Stab stitch; Stem-stitch filling; Stem stitch; Straight stitch; Twisted straight-stitch; Whipped stem-stitch

TO REFRESH YOUR MEMORY

- Before you start *pages 23-28*
- Keeping your work clean and useful hints *page 29*
- Stitches and techniques *pages 31-49*

together to form the shape of the leaf. Work over the pink roses, which will be added on top later.

5. Make the tulips: Use ribbon **5** and, starting at the base on the stem, work three or four ribbon stitches to form the petals. Stitch over the spare tapestry needle, lifting it up to raise the stitch off the surface of the design. Allow the stitches to overlap each other and use a gentle tension whilst you stitch. Use thread **e** and tiny stab stitches to secure the tip of each petal and to re-shape the edges of the outer petals.

6. Make the roses: Use ribbon **6** and make a two-wrap French knot for the centre of the rose. Form the petals in ribbon stitch (see ribbon-stitch rose). Use thread **e** and tiny stab stitches to secure the tips of the petals.

7. Embellish the initial: Use thread **b** and outline the initial in stem stitch to create a soft lilac shadow. Use thread **c** and the same stitch to create the dark shadow on the inside edge of the initial. Change to thread **f** and add another row of stem or back stitch along the edge, here and there, to add the silver highlights.

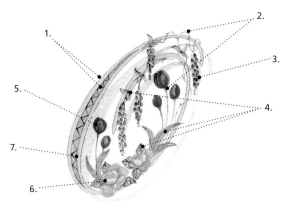

1. Fill in the top curve of the initial: Use thread **a** and fill in the curved yellow section from A to B. Use stem-stitch filling, making the rows close together for a smooth texture. The stitches are 5 mm ($^3/_{16}$ in.) long on the straight bits and 3 mm ($^1/_8$ in.) on the curves. Fill in the gaps with straight stitch. See page 32.

2. Fill in the pattern on the initial: Use thread **a** and start at the rounded end at C. Fill in the yellow block on the rounded end in satin stitch (see satin stitch for blocks on page 56). Fill in the rectangular yellow block in buttonhole stitch and the triangles in buttonhole stitch quarter-wheels. Change to thread **c** and do the same with the pink shapes.

Change to thread **b** and use straight stitch to make the blue edges on the shapes. Use two or three tiny straight stitches formed close together for the blue dots on the yellow blocks. Make a three-wrap French knot on each pink triangle.

3. Make the iris leaves and stems: Use ribbon **1** and twisted straight or ribbon stitch. To form thin stems, twist the ribbon a few times; for wider leaves, twist only once or twice. Where the leaf or stem is behind the initial, insert needle to the back and come up on the other side of the initial. Use thread **d** and straight stitch to re-shape and secure the leaves. To close up the holes at the tip of the leaves, use the same thread and straight stitch.

4. Make the irises: Use ribbon **2** and make the top upright petals first. Use detached chain-stitch, working from the centre upwards. Add one or two ribbon stitches on either side of the detached chain to fill in the shape. Use thread **c** and tiny stab stitches on the tips to re-shape and secure the stitches so they won't be pulled out of shape when you form the adjoining petals. Form the bottom section in detached chain-stitch, working from the centre downwards. Make the two side petals in ribbon stitch, working from the centre outwards.

THREAD

a) Chameleon stranded silk no. 23
b) Chameleon stranded silk no. 19
c) Chameleon stranded silk fynbos no. 3
d) Chameleon stranded silk no. 47
e) Chameleon stranded silk no. 68

Note: use one strand of thread unless suggested otherwise.

RIBBONS

1) Di van Niekerk's 4mm silk no. 31
2) Di van Niekerk's 7mm silk no. 92
3) Di van Niekerk's 4mm silk no. 123

NEEDLES

Crewel size 8 or 9; Chenille size 18, 20 and 24; Tapestry size 13 or 16; Crewel size 10 or straw size 9 for beading

WHAT ELSE?

• printed or traced design
• window fabric
• small seed beads: yellow
• backing fabric
• 10 inch (25 cm) hoop

STITCHES USED (SEE STITCH GALLERY PAGES 52-58)

Buttonhole stitch; Buttonhole stitch: quarter wheel; Outline stitch; Ribbon stitch; Satin stitch for blocks; Stem-stitch filling; Stem stitch; Straight stitch; Twisted ribbon-stitch; Twisted straight-stitch

TO REFRESH YOUR MEMORY

• Before you start *pages 23-28*
• Keeping your work clean and useful hints *page 29*
• Stitches and techniques *pages 31-49*
• Attaching a bead *page 38*

Change to thread **a** and make two-wrap French knots in the centre.

5. Make the forget-me-nots: Form the green stems. Use all six strands of thread **d** on a size 24 chenille needle. Couch the thread in place with one strand of the same thread **d** on a size 8 or 9 crewel needle, spacing the stitches about 4 mm (¹⁄₈ in.) apart. Form the leaves in ribbon **1** and ribbon stitch. Use thread **d** and tiny straight stitches to secure the tips of the leaves. Add a yellow bead in the centre of the flower. Change to ribbon **3** and use loose/puffed ribbon stitches for the blue petals; secure the tip of the petals with thread **b** and a stab stitch.

6. Embellish the initial: Use thread **b** and outline the one blue edge of the initial from C to D and from D to B. Use stem or outline stitch to create a blue shadow. Make a second row alongside if you prefer a thicker blue line. Change to thread **e** and use the same stitch to

make the grey shadows on all the remaining edges of the embroidered initial.

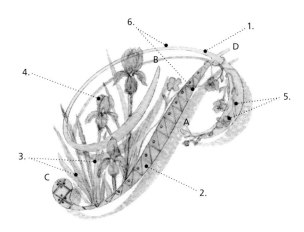

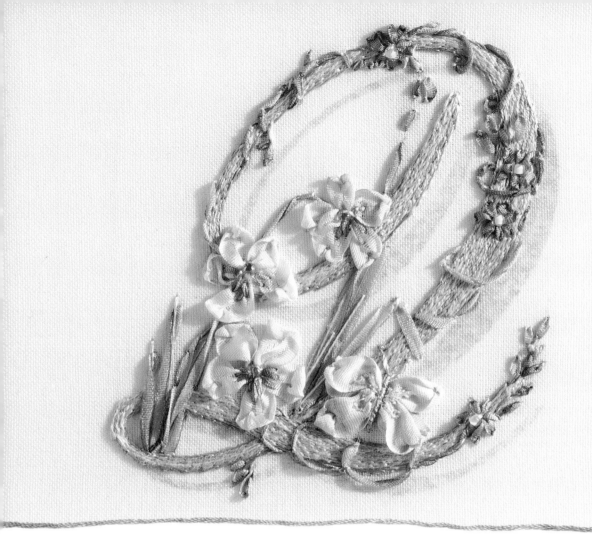

1. **Fill in the initial:** Use thread **a** and make rows of chain stitch close together. Make small chains about 3 mm (¹/₈ in.) in length, working over the flowers and leaves. After three or four rows, change to thread **b**, and make a row of green chain stitch for an interesting effect, then change back to thread **a** again.

2. **Make the twirled stems and small leaves:** Use the template as a guide and form the thin twirled stems in ribbon **1**. Twist the ribbon before couching it in place with thread **b**. Hold the twisted ribbon with your free hand as you couch it and use a gentle tension so as not to flatten the ribbon. Use the spare tapestry needle to gently push the couched ribbon into shape so that the stems have soft curves. Use ribbon **1** for the green leaves and ribbon **2** for the lilac leaves in straight or ribbon stitch. Use thread **b** and tiny stab stitches at the base of the stitches to form the leaf stalks.

3. **Make the upright stems and leaves:** Use ribbon **1** and form the straight or upright stems and leaves of the pansy in twisted ribbon or straight stitch. Start at the base and work upwards. The folded leaf is formed in folded straight-stitch. Use thread **b** and tiny stab stitches to secure the folded section. Use the same thread and straight stitch on some of the leaves and tiny stab stitches along the edge of others to secure the upright leaves in place.

4. **Make the lilac daisies:** Use ribbon **2** and work over the stitches on the initial. Use straight stitch to form narrow, pointed petals and ribbon stitch to form a slightly wider petal with a rounded tip. Alternate between the two stitches and instead of ending off, wrap the lilac ribbon under and over the green stem for an interesting effect. Add a yellow bead in the centre of each daisy.

THREAD

a) Gumnut Aztecs Agate (light)

b) Chameleon stranded cotton no. 36

c) Chameleon stranded silk no. 68

d) Kreinik blending filament no. 032 pearl

Note: use one strand of thread unless suggested otherwise.

RIBBONS

1) Di van Niekerk's 2mm silk no. 25

2) Di van Niekerk's 2mm silk no. 73

3) Di van Niekerk's 7mm silk no. 128

4) Di van Niekerk's 7mm silk no. 52

NEEDLES

Crewel size 8 or 9; Chenille size 18 and 22; Tapestry size 13 or 16; Crewel size 10 or straw size 9 for beading

WHAT ELSE?

- printed or traced design
- window fabric
- small seed beads: yellow and lilac
- backing fabric
- 10 inch (25 cm) hoop

STITCHES USED (SEE STITCH GALLERY PAGES 52-58)

Couching; Folded straight-stitch; Padded ribbon-stitch; Ribbon stitch; Split back-stitch; Stab stitch; Stem stitch; Straight stitch; Twisted ribbon-stitch; Twisted straight-stitch

TO REFRESH YOUR MEMORY

- Before you start *pages 23-28*
- Keeping your work clean and useful hints *page 29*
- Stitches and techniques *pages 31-49*
- Attaching a bead *page 38*

5. Make the yellow pansies: Use ribbon **4** and ribbon stitch for each petal; work from the centre outwards. Secure the stitch at the base with thread **b** so that it doesn't pull out of shape when you make the adjoining petals. Use ribbon **2** and a straight stitch to form the stripes on the petals. Add a lilac bead in the centre of the pansy.

6. Make the butterfly: Make the body with thread **c** and whipped back-stitch. Make three or four 3 mm (1/8 in.) back stitches and whip each stitch several times. Make the antennae with a pistil stitch. Use ribbon **3** and form the four wings in padded ribbon-stitch, working from the body outwards. Hold the stitch in place as you take the needle to the back of your work. Use thread **c** and tiny stab stitches to secure each wing along the tip and base before forming the next wing. Change to thread **d** and add a few straight or pistil stitches at the base of each wing.

7. Add more detail: Use thread **c** and add a grey shadow along the bottom edge of the initial in split back-stitch or stem stitch. Work close to the edge of the initial.

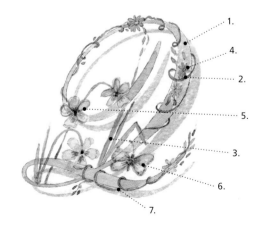

1. **Outline the initial:** Use thread **a** and back stitch or split back-stitch to outline the initial. See outlining an initial on page 32.

2. **Make the red pattern on the initial:** Use thread **b** and straight stitch to form the zigzag pattern on the initial. Secure the stitches in place at each intersection with a tiny stab stitch.

3. **Add the beads:** Use thread **b** to secure red beads on the initial as shown in the photograph.

4. **Make the curled stem around the initial:** Use ribbon **1**, twist it and couch it in place with thread **a**, spacing the stitches 2 to 4 mm ($^1/_{16}$ to $^1/_8$ in.) apart.

5. **Make the upright stems of the tulips and leaves:** Use thread **a** and chain stitch to form the straight stems; wrap ribbon **1** or **2** around the chain stitches (see whipped chain-stitch page 58). For fine stems, wrap the chain stitch with the same thread. Alternatively, use

THREAD

a) Gumnut "Stars" pure silk no. 466 turquoise

b) Gumnut "Stars" pure silk no. 178 mulberry

Note: use one strand of thread unless suggested otherwise.

RIBBONS

1) Di van Niekerk's 2mm silk no. 69

2) Di van Niekerk's 2mm silk no. 29

3) Di van Niekerk's 4mm silk no. 30

4) Di van Niekerk's 7mm silk no. 59

NEEDLES

Crewel size 8 or 9; Chenille size 18, 20 and 22;
Tapestry size 13 or 16

WHAT ELSE?

- printed or traced design
- window fabric
- small red glass seed beads
- backing fabric
- 10 inch (25 cm) hoop

STITCHES USED (SEE STITCH GALLERY PAGES 52-58)

Back stitch; Couching; Detached chain-stitch; French knot;
Overcast stitch; Pistil stitch; Ribbon stitch with curled-up tips;
Split back-stitch; Stab stitch; Stem stitch; Straight stitch; Twisted
ribbon-stitch; Twisted straight-stitch; Whipped chain-stitch

TO REFRESH YOUR MEMORY

- Before you start *pages 23-28*
- Keeping your work clean and useful hints *page 29*
- Stitches and techniques *pages 31-49*
- Attaching a bead *page 38*

ribbon **3** and twisted straight-stitch. Secure the stitch with thread **a** and tiny stab stitches.

6. Make the long leaves: Use ribbon **3** and twisted ribbon or straight-stitch. Secure the ribbon in place with thread **a** and tiny stab stitches. Form the curled-up tips in pistil or stem stitch.

7. Make the small teardrop-shaped leaves: Use ribbon **2** for the small leaves and ribbon **3** for the larger ones in ribbon or detached chain-stitch.

8. Make the red tulips: Use ribbon no. **4** and ribbon stitch with curled up tips. Work the left and right petals first, then add a third petal in the middle, overlapping the first two petals. Use thread **b** to secure the stitches in place with tiny stab stitches.

9. Add red detail: Make two-wrap French knots between the leaves in thread **b**, then wrap the thread under and over the stems to add more colour.

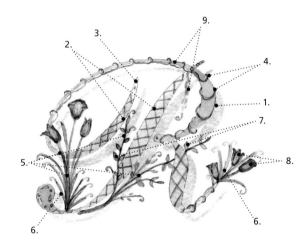

1. Decorate the initial: The initial is not filled in with stitches, but it is decorated with stitches for an interesting effect. Use ribbon **1** and straight stitch to form the green lines on the initial. Use thread **a** and a tiny stab stitch at each intersection to secure the lines in place. Change to thread **b** and a three-wrap French knot to form the pink dots on the initial.

2. Form the stems: Use ribbon **1** and twist the ribbon before couching it in place to form the twirled stems. Use thread **a** to couch the ribbon, spacing the stitches 2 to 4 mm ($^1/_{16}$ to $^1/_8$ in.) apart.

3. Make the leaves: Work the green leaves in ribbon **1** using ribbon or straight stitch over a spare tapestry needle to raise the stitch up off the surface of the design.

4. Make the blue daisies: Use ribbon **2** and ribbon stitch for the small petals. Change to detached chain-stitch for the larger petals. Work from the centre of the daisy outwards. Using thread **a** or **b**, add a three-wrap French knot in the centre.

5. Make the pink flowers: Use ribbon **3** and a loop stitch for each flower. Work over a spare tapestry needle to form a raised loop. Use thread **b** and flatten the loop with your fingertip as you make a three-wrap French knot on the loop to form the centre of the flower.

6. Add the pink detail: Use thread **b** and straight or

THREAD

▨▨▨▨▨▨▨ a) Gumnut "Stars" pure silk no. 604 green

▨▨▨▨▨▨▨ b) Gumnut "Stars" pure silk no. 095 pink

Note: use one strand of thread unless suggested otherwise.

RIBBONS

▬▬▬▬▬ 1) Di van Niekerk's 2mm silk no. 80

▬▬▬▬▬ 2) Di van Niekerk's 2mm silk no. 68

▬▬▬▬▬ 3) Di van Niekerk's 7mm silk no. 114

NEEDLES

Crewel size 8 or 9; Chenille mixed pack size 18 /24;
Tapestry size 18

WHAT ELSE?

• printed or traced design
• backing fabric
• window fabric
• 10 inch (25 cm) hoop

STITCHES USED (SEE STITCH GALLERY PAGES 52-58)

Back stitch; Couching; Detached chain-stitch; French knot;
Loop stitch; Pistil stitch; Ribbon stitch; Running stitch;
Split back stitch; Stab stitch; Straight stitch

TO REFRESH YOUR MEMORY

• Before you start *pages 23-28*
• Keeping your work clean and useful hints *page 29*
• Stitches and techniques *pages 31-49*

pistil stitch to form the pink petals between the green leaves. Outline the initial in the same thread, using back or split back-stitch.

7. Enhance the shadow: Use thread **a** and running stitch along the edge of the shadow to enhance the initial.

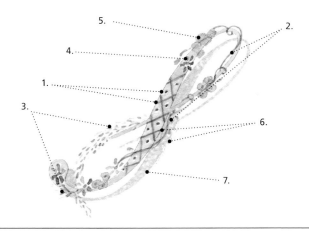

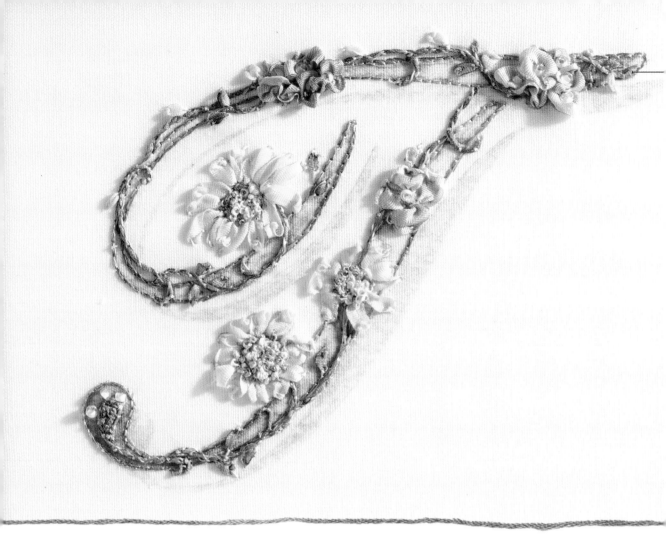

1. Outline the initial: Use thread **a** and outline the initial in back stitch. Make small stitches about 3 mm (¹/₈ in.) in length and use shorter stitches to accommodate the curves. See page 32.

2. Make the stems and leaves: Use ribbon **1** and twist it slightly before couching it in place with thread **b**. Space the stitches approximately 5 mm (³/₁₆ in.) apart, making them closer together on the curves. Use a gentle tension so as not to flatten the ribbon. Make the leaves with ribbon **1** and use a ribbon or straight stitch. Work over the size 22 tapestry needle to form raised stitches. Use thread **b** and tiny stab stitches at the base and tip of the leaf to secure the stitch in place.

3. Make the yellow daisies: Use ribbon **2** and twisted ribbon or straight stitch for the yellow petals. Work from the centre outwards and stitch over the tapestry needle to form a slightly raised petal. Use thread **c** and tiny stab stitches at the base and tip of the petals to secure the stitch in place. To form the centre of the daisy, use thread **b** and a three-wrap French knot on the green sections, thread **c** and the same stitch on the yellow sections. Use thread **a** or **d** and the same stitch to form the dark shadows on the edge of the round centre.

4. Make the purple flowers: Use ribbon **3** and loop stitch or loose and puffed ribbon stitch to form the petals. Work over the large tapestry needle to form raised petals. Use thread **c** and secure a yellow bead in the centre of the flower.

5. Make the lilac flowers: Use ribbon **4** and the same stitch as above for the lilac flowers. Add a yellow bead in the centre.

6. Embellish the initial: Use thread **d** and wrap it around the green stems to add a touch of colour. See whipped couching on page 58. Insert the needle under

THREAD

	a) Chameleon stranded silk no. 66
	b) Chameleon stranded silk no. 61
	c) Chameleon stranded silk no. 12
	d) Chameleon stranded cotton no. 38
	e) Madeira metallic 40 no. 4 gold

Note: use one strand of thread unless suggested otherwise.

RIBBONS

	1) Di van Niekerk's 2mm silk no. 24
	2) Di van Niekerk's 4mm silk no. 55
	3) Di van Niekerk's 7mm silk no. 40
	4) Di van Niekerk's 7mm silk no. 74

NEEDLES

Crewel size 9 or 10; Chenille size 18, 20 and 22; Tapestry size 16 or 13 and 22; Crewel size 10 or straw size 9 for beading

WHAT ELSE?

- printed or traced design
- backing fabric
- window fabric
- 10 inch (25 cm) hoop
- small seed beads: yellow

STITCHES USED (SEE STITCH GALLERY PAGES 52-58)

Back stitch; Couching; French knot; Ribbon stitch; Stab stitch; Stem stitch; Straight stitch; Twisted ribbon-stitch; Twisted straight-stitch; Whipped couching

TO REFRESH YOUR MEMORY

- Before you start *pages 23-28*
- Keeping your work clean and useful hints *page 29*
- Stitches and techniques *pages 31-49*
- Attaching a bead *page 38*

and over the couched stem. For gold highlights use thread **e** and repeat the process. Add three yellow beads on the curved end at A; use thread **d** or **c** to secure the beads in place. Use thread **d** and three-wrap French knots inside the purple comma-shape at A. Outline sections of the initial in thread **d** to add more colour, using back or stem stitch alongside the stitches that you made in step 1. Use thread **e** and add gold highlights along the edge of the initial in back stitch to create a rich texture. Use ribbon **2** and ribbon stitch to make the yellow leaves leading off the stem.

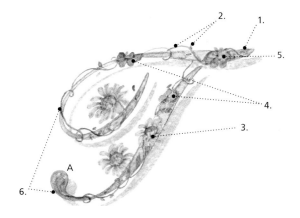

1. Fill in the initial: Use one or two strands of thread **a** and raised stem-stitch. (See raised stem-stitch on page 33.) Change to one strand of thread **b** and outline the edge of the initial in outline or stem stitch.

2. Make the stems: Use ribbon **1** and couching stitch. Twist the ribbon and couch it in place with thread **c**. Use tiny stab stitches to re-shape the stem if necessary.

3. Make the roses and buds: Use ribbon **2** and ribbon stitch. Change to thread **d** and secure each stitch at the base with tiny stab stitches. Make a few three-wrap French knots in the centre of the open roses.

4. Make the leaves: Use ribbon **1** and detached chain-stitch for the slender, elongated leaves, fly stitch for the large leaves, and ribbon stitch for the small leaves

5. Make the green calyx: Use ribbon **1** and ribbon or fly stitch to form the green calyx on the buds.

THREAD

	a) Gumnut "Stars" pure silk no. 193
	b) Chameleon stranded silk no. 66
	c) Chameleon stranded silk no. 54
	d) Chameleon stranded silk no. 37
	e) Any fine silver metallic thread

Note: use one strand of thread unless suggested otherwise.

RIBBONS

	1) Di van Niekerk's 4mm silk no. 16
	2) Di van Niekerk's 7mm silk no. 37

NEEDLES

Crewel size 8 or 9; Chenille size 18 and 20;
Tapestry size 13 or 16

WHAT ELSE?

- printed or traced design
- backing fabric
- window fabric
- 10 inch (25 cm) hoop

STITCHES USED (SEE STITCH GALLERY PAGES 52-58)

Couching; Detached chain-stitch; Fly stitch; French knot;
Outline stitch; Raised stem-stitch; Ribbon stitch; Stab stitch;
Stem stitch; Whipped couching

TO REFRESH YOUR MEMORY

- Before you start *pages 23-28*
- Keeping your work clean and useful hints *page 29*
- Stitches and techniques *pages 31-49*

6. Optional add-ons: Make the silver highlights:
Use thread **e** and work slanted straight stitches over the
embroidered initial. Whip some stems with the same
thread. See whipped couching on page 58.

7. Optional add-ons: Make the gold highlights: Use
thread **d** and whip some of the couched green stems to
add more colour.

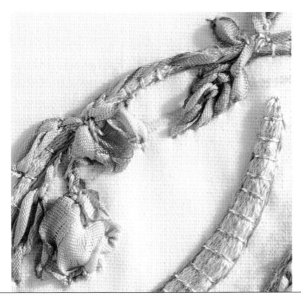

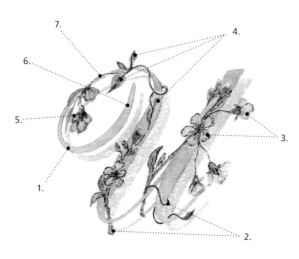

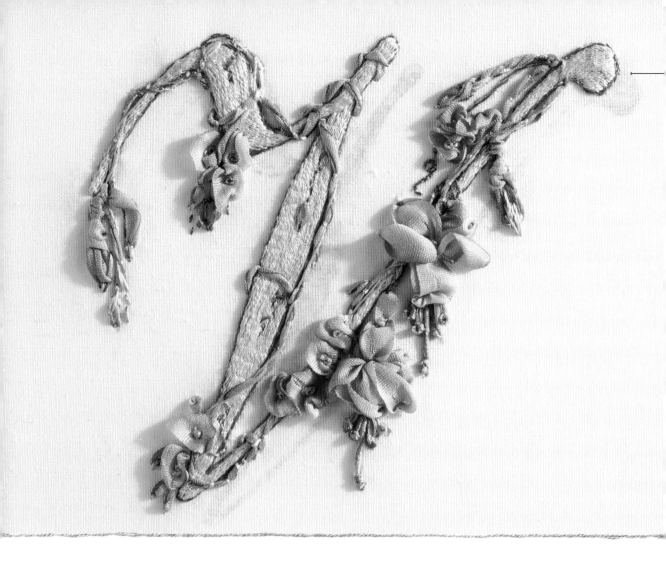

1. **Fill in the initial:** Form the foundation stitches for raised stem-stitch in thread **a**. Work horizontal stitches from side to side, spaced about 3 to 4 mm (¹/₈ in.) apart. Pull them quite taut and use an even tension. Work over the flowers, leaves and stems. Use the same thread **a** for the raised stem-stitch, pushing the stitches close together with your fingertip as you form each subsequent row (see page 33). Outline the initial in thread **b** in stem or back stitch to create a shadow and to neaten the edge.

2. **Form the stems:** Use ribbon **1** and couch the ribbon in place with thread **c**, spacing the stitches 4 mm (¹/₈ in.) apart. Where the stem lies behind the initial, take the needle and ribbon to the back and come up on the other side of the initial. Use the same thread and tiny stab stitches to re-shape the ribbon into smooth curves where necessary. Form the thin dark tendrils in thread **b** using back stitch. Work over the pink stitches.

3. **Make the round flowers:** Use ribbon **2** for the round lilac flowers and ribbon **4** for the round pink flowers. Use a loop stitch, working over the spare tapestry needle. Add a three-wrap French knot in the centre, using thread **a** or **d**.

4. **Make the fuchsias:** Use ribbon **3** and pistil stitch to form the long pink stamens of the fuchsia. Change to ribbon **2** and use loose, puffed ribbon stitch for the lilac skirt of the fuchsia. Work with a loose tension, over the spare tapestry needle for a raised effect and add another stitch or two on top for a fuller skirt. Use thread **a** and tiny stab stitches to secure the tips of the stitches in place so that they don't pull out of shape as you stitch. Use ribbon **4** to form the pink petals in ribbon stitch, twisting the ribbon to form the curled petals. Work over the spare tapestry needle and use a gentle tension. Use thread **a** and tiny stab stitches to secure

THREAD

	a) Gumnut "Stars" pure silk no. 073
	b) Chameleon stranded cotton or silk no. 8
	c) Chameleon stranded cotton or silk no. 61
	d) Chameleon stranded silk no. 37

Note: use one strand of thread unless suggested otherwise.

RIBBONS

	1) Di van Niekerk's 4mm silk no. 132
	2) Di van Niekerk's 7mm silk no. 74
	3) Di van Niekerk's 2mm silk no. 112
	4) Di van Niekerk's 7mm silk no. 41

NEEDLES

Crewel size 8 or 9; Chenille size 18, 20 and 22; Tapestry size 13

WHAT ELSE?

- printed or traced design
- backing fabric
- window fabric
- 10 inch (25 cm) hoop

STITCHES USED (SEE STITCH GALLERY PAGES 52-58)

Back stitch; French knot; Grab stitch; Loop stitch; Loose/puffed ribbon stitch; Padded ribbon-stitch; Pistil stitch; Raised stem-stitch; Ribbon stitch; Stab stitch; Stem stitch; Straight stitch; Twisted ribbon-stitch; Whipped back-stitch

TO REFRESH YOUR MEMORY

- Before you start *pages 23-28*
- Keeping your work clean and useful hints *page 29*
- Stitches and techniques *pages 31-49*

---

the tips of the petals in place. Change to thread **b** and use tiny stab stitches to re-shape the pistil stitches.

5. Make the fuchsia buds: Use ribbon **4** and ribbon or straight stitch for the pink buds. Secure the tip of the bud with thread **a** or **b** and a stab stitch or two. Change to ribbon **1** and use a grab stitch at the base of the bud and make two back stitches about 4 mm (¹/₈ in.) in length. Whip the back stitches to form the thick green sections just above the fuchsias.

6. Make the leaves: Use ribbon **1** and ribbon stitch for the leaves. Use thread **c** to secure the tips of the leaves with a stab stitch. Change to thread **b** and add a few straight stitches between the leaves.

7. Add golden yellow detail: Use thread **d** and make a three-wrap French knot in the centre of some of the round flowers to add more colour. Loosely whip some green stems with the same thread. Add a few straight

stitches at the tip of one bud; make a few straight stitches between the leaves for colour.

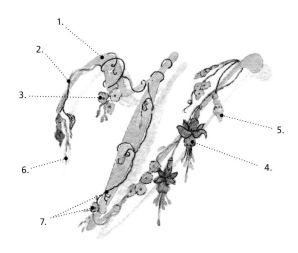

1. Fill in the initial: Use thread **a** and fill in the initial with rows of stem stitch. Make the rows close together for a smooth finish and make short stitches on the curve; fill in the gaps with straight stitch. See stem-stitch filling on page 32. Use thread **b** and stem stitch along the edge of the initial to create a dark shadow and to neaten the edge at the same time.

2. Make the stems: Use thread **b** and stem or back stitch for the twirled stems of the daisies, making short stitches on the curves. Use two or three rows of stem stitch close together for the upright stems of the lilies.

3. Make the daisies and leaves: Use ribbon **1** and detached chain-stitch for the leaves. Use thread **b** and a grab stitch at the base of each leaf to form a neat, narrow leaf; insert the needle further away to create a short, slender stalk. Use ribbon **2** and ribbon or straight stitch for the daisy petals, working over the spare tapestry needle. Use thread **a** or **b** and add a yellow bead in the centre of each daisy.

4. Make the orange lilies: Use ribbon **3** and three or four straight stitches formed at an angle to make the trumpet part of the lily. Work from the stem upwards. Use thread **b** and make two or three straight stitches on top to create the dark shadows.

THREAD

▓▓▓▓▓	a) Gumnut "Stars" pure silk no. 784
▓▓▓▓▓	b) Chameleon stranded silk no. 111

Note: use one strand of thread unless suggested otherwise.

RIBBONS

▓▓▓▓▓	1) Di van Niekerk's 2mm silk no. 35
▓▓▓▓▓	2) Di van Niekerk's 2mm silk no. 81
▓▓▓▓▓	3) Di van Niekerk's 2mm silk no. 109
▓▓▓▓▓	4) Di van Niekerk's 7mm silk no. 57
▓▓▓▓▓	5) Di van Niekerk's 7mm silk no. 16

NEEDLES

Crewel size 9 or 10; Chenille size 18 and 22; Tapestry size 18; Crewel size 10 or straw size 9 for beading

WHAT ELSE?

- printed or traced design
- backing fabric
- window fabric
- 10 inch (25 cm) hoop
- small glass seed beads: yellow

STITCHES USED (SEE STITCH GALLERY PAGES 52-58)

Back stitch; Detached chain-stitch; French knot; Grab stitch; Ribbon stitch; Stab stitch; Stem-stitch filling; Stem stitch; Straight stitch; Twisted ribbon-stitch; Twisted straight-stitch

TO REFRESH YOUR MEMORY

- Before you start *pages 23-28*
- Keeping your work clean and useful hints *page 29*
- Stitches and techniques *pages 31-49*
- Attaching a bead *page 38*

Change to ribbon **4** and make the orange petals in ribbon stitch, working from the centre outwards and stitching over the spare tapestry needle. Use thread **b** and tiny stab stitches to form the dark dots at the base of the petal. Use the same thread and stitch to form the brown outer tips.

Use ribbon **3** and two straight stitches to form the yellow stamens in the centre of each lily. Change to thread **b** and use two-wrap French knots to add more dots on the petals. Use straight stitch to make the dark shadows between the stamens.

5. Make the lily leaves: Change to ribbon **5** and use twisted straight- or ribbon-stitch to form the long leaves. Use thread **b** and a few stab stitches at the tip and the base of each leaf to secure the stitch. Folding the ribbon in half with your index finger, use a tiny stab stitch or two along the edge to hold the shape of the ribbon.

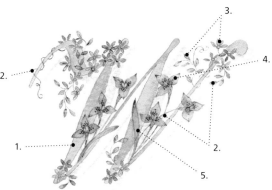

1. Fill in the initial: Use one or two strands of thread **a** and fill in the initial in raised stem-stitch. See more about raised stem-stitch on page 33. Outline the edge of the initial in thread **b** and split back-stitch or stem stitch.

2. Make the stems: Use ribbon **1** and twist the ribbon before couching it in place with thread **a**. Use a gentle tension so as not to flatten the ribbon.

3. Make the large pink roses: Use ribbon **4** to form a golden yellow centre with a one-wrap French knot. Thread up with ribbon **2** and make two large pink fly-stitch roses. Add two or three ribbon stitches on top of the fly stitches to form the open petals at the base of the rose.

4. Make the pink rosebuds: Use ribbon **4** and make the yellow centre of the bud in a French knot as you did in step 3. Change to ribbon **2** and make a fly stitch around the yellow centre to form the pink bud. Use

THREAD

a) Gumnut "Stars" pure silk no. 466

b) Gumnut "Stars" pure silk no. 193

c) Silver metallic thread

Note: use one strand of thread unless suggested otherwise.

RIBBONS

1) Di van Niekerk's 2mm silk no. 28

2) Di van Niekerk's 7mm silk no. 43

3) Di van Niekerk's 4mm silk no. 27

4) Di van Niekerk's 4mm silk no. 109

NEEDLES

Crewel size 8 or 9; Chenille size 22, 20, and 16; Tapestry size 13

WHAT ELSE?

- printed or traced design
- backing fabric
- window fabric
- 10 inch (25 cm) hoop

STITCHES USED (SEE STITCH GALLERY PAGES 52-58)

Couching; Fly stitch; Fly-stitch rose; French knot; Loop stitch; Pistil stitch; Raised stem-stitch; Ribbon stitch; Split back-stitch; Stem stitch; Straight stitch

TO REFRESH YOUR MEMORY

- Before you start *pages 23-28*
- Keeping your work clean and useful hints *page 29*
- Stitches and techniques *pages 31-49*

thread **b** to re-shape the stitches and to secure the tails at the back of your work.

5. **Make the leaves and calyx of the buds:** Use ribbon **3** and ribbon stitch for the leaves. Form the green calyx on top of the buds in ribbon **1**, using ribbon stitch.

6. **Make the pink lines and dots at the leaves and stems:** Use ribbon **2** and straight stitch for the larger pink dots, use thread **b** and French knots for the tiny dots. Use pistil stitch or straight stitch for the thin, longer pink lines alongside the stem.

7. **Make the yellow flowers:** Use ribbon **4** and loop stitch to form the yellow flowers. Work over the spare tapestry needle when forming the loops. Secure each loop in place with thread **a**. Use a three-wrap French knot forming the flower centre at the same time.

8. **Add-ons: Make the silver and pink highlights:** Use thread **c** and work slanted straight stitches over the raised initial. Whip the stems with thread **b**.

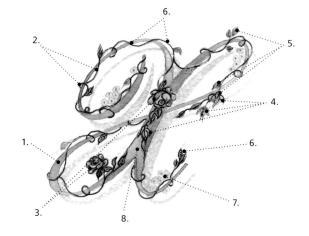

1. Fill in the initial: Use two strands of thread **a** and form the foundation stitches for raised stem-stitch. Work horizontal stitches from side to side and space them about 3 mm (⅛ in.) apart. Pull the stitches quite taut and use an even tension. Work over the roses, leaves and stems. Use two strands of the same thread **a** for the raised stem-stitch, pushing the stitches close together with your fingertip as you form the subsequent rows (see page 33).

2. Make the stems: Use thread **b** and whipped back- or stem-stitch to form the twirled green stem. Work over the embroidered initial using the watercolour as a guide. The back stitches are about 3 mm (⅛ in.) long but are shorter when you reach the curves. Wrap the thread back and forth under and over the back stitches to form the thicker stems. For very fine stems there is no need to whip the stitches.

3. Make the pink daises: Use ribbon **1** and form the pink petals in ribbon or straight stitch, working from the centre outwards. Stitch over a spare tapestry needle to create raised stitches. Use thread **b** and tiny stab stitches to make the green calyx on the opened buds and use two-wrap French knots made close together for larger patches of green. Use a tiny stab stitch to secure the tip of the petals so they don't pull out of shape later. Add a bead in the centre of the daisy.

4. Make the leaves: Use ribbon **2** and ribbon or straight stitch to form the green leaves, working from the stem outwards. Use ribbon **1** and the same stitch for the pink leaves. Change to thread **b** and use a stab stitch at the tip of the leaves to secure the stitch in place.

5. Make the pansies: Use ribbon **3** and loose/puffed ribbon stitch to form the pansy petals working from the centre outwards. Use thread **a** and tiny stab stitches to

THREAD

a) Gumnut "Stars" pure silk no. 365
b) Gumnut "Stars" pure silk no. 587
c) Any fine silver metallic thread

Note: use one strand of thread unless suggested otherwise.

RIBBONS

1) Di van Niekerk's 2mm silk ribbon no. 41
2) Di van Niekerk's 2mm silk ribbon no. 36
3) Di van Niekerk's 7mm silk ribbon no. 74

NEEDLES

Crewel size 9; Chenille size 22 and 18; Tapestry size 18; Crewel size 10 or straw size 9 for beading

WHAT ELSE?

- printed or traced design
- backing fabric
- window fabric
- 10 inch (25 cm) hoop
- small seed beads: dark blue and pale yellow

STITCHES USED (SEE STITCH GALLERY PAGES 52-58)

Back stitch; Raised stem-stitch; Ribbon stitch; Loose/puffed ribbon stitch; Split back-stitch; Stab stitch; Stem stitch; Straight stitch; Whipped back-stitch; Whipped stem-stitch

TO REFRESH YOUR MEMORY

- Before you start *pages 23-28*
- Keeping your work clean and useful hints *page 29*
- Stitches and techniques *pages 31-49*
- Attaching a bead *page 38*

re-shape and secure each petal along the rounded tips. Use tiny straight stitches at the base of each stitch to flatten it and to create the veins on the petal. Add two or three yellow beads in the centre.

6. Add more detail: Use thread **b** and stem stitch or split back-stitch along one edge of the initial to create a dark shadow and use thread **c** and the same stitch along the opposite edge to create highlights. Use the same thread **c** and whip some stems for added highlights. Use a gentle tension inserting the needle under and over the green stems.

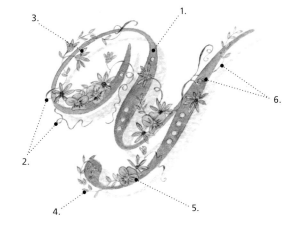

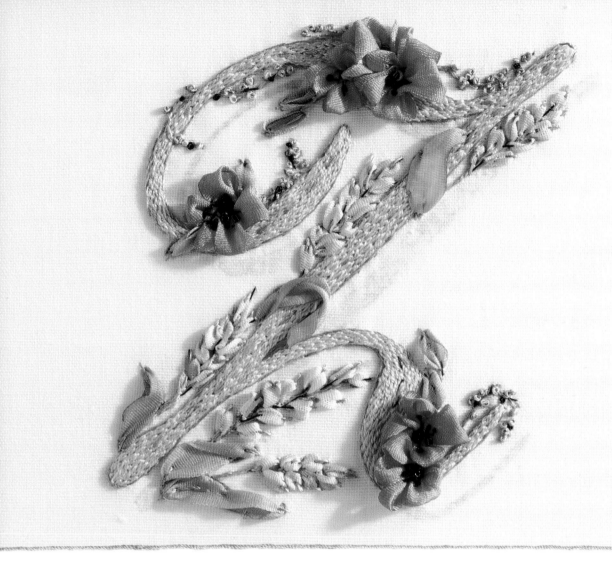

1. Fill in the initial: Use thread **a** and chain stitch to fill in the initial. Work off the hoop and make row after row of chain stitch. The chain stitches are about 3 mm (¹/₈ in.) in length. See chain-stitch filling on page 35. Change to thread **b** or **c** and outline the initial in stem or split back-stitch. Use two strands of thread **b** and straight stitch to make the small stripes on top of the chain stitches on the initial.

2. Embroider the stems: Use thread **b** or **c** and stem or split back-stitch to form the thin stems.

3. Embroider the seeds: For the tiny round seeds use two- or three-wrap French knots in thread **b** for the cinnamon-brown seeds, thread **c** for the darker brown ones. For the ears of corn use ribbon **1** and straight stitch worked over a spare tapestry needle. Change to

THREAD

 a) Gumnut "Stars" pure silk no. 746

b) Chameleon stranded silk no. 109

c) Chameleon stranded cotton no. 25

d) Rajmahal Art.Silk no. 29

Note: use one strand of thread unless suggested otherwise.

RIBBONS

1) Di van Niekerk's 4mm silk no. 110

2) Di van Niekerk's 7mm silk no. 36

3) Di van Niekerk's 7mm silk no. 87

NEEDLES

Crewel size 9 or 10; Chenille size 18 and 20; Tapestry size 18; Crewel size 10 or straw size 9 for beading

WHAT ELSE?

- printed or traced design
- backing fabric
- window fabric
- 10 inch (25 cm) hoop
- small seed beads: black

STITCHES USED (SEE STITCH GALLERY PAGES 52-58)

Chain-stitch filling; Chain stitch; French knot; Split back-stitch; Stab stitch; Stem stitch; Straight stitch; Twisted straight-stitch

TO REFRESH YOUR MEMORY

- Before you start *pages 23-28*
- Keeping your work clean and useful hints *page 29*
- Stitches and techniques *pages 31-49*
- Attaching a bead *page 38*

thread **c** and form the dark shadows working a straight stitch at the base and tip of each stitch.

4. Embroider the leaves: Use ribbon **2** and twisted straight-stitch to form the large green leaves and straight stitch for the smaller leaves. Use thread **c** and tiny stab stitches to re-shape and secure the stitch along the edge, base and tip of the leaf.

5. Embroider the poppies: Working from the centre outwards, use ribbon **3** and four or five loop stitches to form the petals of each poppy. Stitch over the spare tapestry needle when forming the loop. Use thread **d** and tiny stab stitches at the base of the stitch to secure the loop in place and make two-wrap French knots to form the black dots in the centre. Add one or more small black seed bead in the middle of the flower.

6. Add the black detail: To balance the blackness of the poppy centres, use thread **d** and two-wrap French knots or straight stitch between the brown seeds on the design.

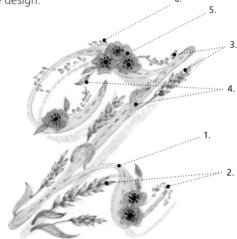

More ideas

'THANK YOU' PLAQUE OR CARD

The template for this is on page 127. Outline the words in two strands of thread using back stitches of about 3 mm (¹/₈ in.) long, but a little shorter on the curves. Whip them with ribbon (see page 47 and 48).

Make the green rose stems with ribbon, twisting it before couching it in place with thread. Make the purple berry stems in stem stitch. For the lilac berries, use ribbon and a French knot, wrapping the ribbon twice around the needle for larger berries and once for the smaller ones. Work the berry leaves in ribbon stitch from the stem outwards and use a tiny stab stitch at the tip of each leaf to secure the stitch in place in thread.

Use one strand of thread for the rose leaves; start at the tip with a straight stitch and proceed with fly or satin stitch, working towards the leaf stalk, the stem or the rose. Fill in the gaps with straight stitch (see satin stitch for leaves on page 56).

Work the dark centre of the light red roses in ribbon and a three-wrap French knot. Use a fly-stitch rose to form the dark, tightly coiled centre. Make three or four fly stitches and work up to and just beyond the wide upright petals, then form the upright and open petals in ribbon stitch with curled-up tips. Allow the stitches to overlap each other and the fly stitch centre. Use tiny stab stitches to add the dark shadows between the petals and to secure the ribbon stitches. Work the dark red roses in the same stitches changing your ribbon and thread colours. The small rosebuds are worked in padded ribbon-stitch, the bigger ones in fly stitch or ribbon stitch with curled-up tips. Use twisted straight or straight stitch to form the green calyx on the large roses in ribbon, working from the stem up, down or outwards. Secure and re-shape the stitches with stab stitches. Repeat for the rosebuds using straight stitch or make one or two fly stitches and add one or more tiny stab stitches at the tip of the stitches for a realistic finish. To form the rounded green knob at the base of some roses and buds, use a grab stitch or make one short back stitch and whip it several times.

'WELCOME' PLAQUE OR CARD

The template for this welcome border is on page 127. First embroider the words in back stitch, about 4 mm (¹/₈ in.) long, but shorter on the curves. Whip the back stitches with ribbon (see page 47 and 48). Whip sections of the word with thread for interesting highlights.

Embroider the wisteria using thread and whipped back-stitch to form the brown branches, then form the leaves in ribbon and ribbon stitch and secure them with tiny stab stitches. Use straight or back stitch at the base of the leaf to form the leaf stalks and work one-wrap French knots in ribbon for the wisteria flowers. Work the remaining green stems and leaves in thread for all the thin stems and ribbon for the thicker stems. Use back, stem, straight, or twisted straight-stitch to form all the stems of the flowers. Form the small leaves in ribbon, using ribbon or straight stitch and working from the stem outwards.

French knots made close together are used for the grape hyacinths – one wrap for the smaller and two wraps for the bigger petals.

Form the yellow flowers, white daisies and the pink lilies in ribbon or straight stitch; use pistil or straight stitch for the stamens, or use a two-wrap French knot in the centre of each flower.

Work the purple petals of the violets in ribbon stitch over a spare tapestry needle to form a raised stitch, working from the centre outwards. Use the same stitch for the pink and yellow petals, and tiny stab stitches at the petal tips to re-shape and secure each stitch. Work the centres in three-wrap French knots.

Use ribbon stitch for the pansies, and straight stitch for the tiny buds. Create the lines in the centre in thread with stab stitch, with blanket stitch along the edge of each white petal to create the pink tips. Use stab stitch for the black stripes, and a three-wrap French knot to form the green dot in the centre.

The poppies are made with a ribbon-stitch rose (see ribbon-stitch rose on page 56). Use a gentle tension, working over a spare tapestry needle to hold the stitch as you take the needle to the back. Use tiny stab stitches to secure the stitch at the base and tip so that it does not pull out of shape as you form the adjoining petals. Add a few black beads or two-wrap French knots to form the centre.

knots in thread for the yellow centre, Make the rose buds in ribbon or straight stitch and the green calyx in straight or fly stitch. The round knob is a grab stitch.

Make the large pink roses working with two needles. Come up in the centre of the rose with a ribbon needle, then repeat with a thread needle. Lay the needle and thread on top of your work. With the pink ribbon, make a two-wrap French knot. Anchor the knot with the pink thread and tiny stab stitches. Lay the needle and thread on top of you work. Make a ribbon-stitch rose working from left to right in a circular form, working over a spare tapestry needle to form a raised stitch. Work ribbon stitches around the knot, starting each stitch halfway back, just above the previous stitch (see ribbon-stitch rose page 56). Some petals are made in ribbon stitch with curled-up tips. Use the needle and thread to secure each stitch at the base and tip with tiny stab stitches so that it won't pull out of shape as you make the next row of petals. Alternate between three shades for a realistic rose. Don't start at the end of the previous ribbon stitch, always work halfway back, above or below the previous stitch and overlap some stitches as shown in the completed project.

Work the yellow rose centres in three-wrap French knots. Make a few single knotted stitches between the French knots and trim them for a fluffy texture.

'I LOVE YOU' CARD

Use the template on page 127. Outline the words in thread in back stitches of about 3 mm (¹/₈ in.) long but a little shorter on the curves. Whip the stitches with ribbon, twice at the wider sections.

Make the stems of the large pink roses in whipped stem-stitch, then form the large rose leaves in ribbon stitch with curled-up tips. Edge the ribbon leaves in blanket stitch, making the stitches at an angle to form the veins of the leaf at the same time. Form the stems of the pink daisies in the same way, then work the leaves in detached chain or ribbon stitch, using tiny stab stitches to re-shape them if necessary. For the pink daisy petals, work padded ribbon-stitch over a spare tapestry needle, securing each stitch at the tip and base with tiny stab stitches so that it doesn't pull out of shape as you form the adjoining petals. Use three-wrap French

BIRTHDAY CARD

Use the template on page 127. Form the words in ribbon in whipped back-stitches of 3 mm (1/8 in.) long, but shorter on the curves. Form the straight lines alongside the words in thread in back or stem stitch.

Make the thick green stems in ribbon and whipped back-stitch, and the thin green stems in thread in a whipped stem or back stitch

Work detached chain from the centre outwards in ribbon to form the pink daisy petals, the buds in twisted straight-stitch working from the green calyx upwards. Form the light green section above the calyx in ribbon in straight stitch, inserting the needle between the pink petals. Make the dark green leaves and the calyx of the buds in ribbon stitch. The yellow centre consists of three-wrap French knots in thread.

Form the leaves of the yellow flowers in ribbon stitch, securing them in place with tiny stab stitches at the tip and base of each leaf.

Work the yellow flowers in detached chain-stitch and use padded ribbon-stitch to form the yellow buds. Change to green thread and add a three-wrap French knot in the centre.

Use ribbon stitch for some petals of the blue flowers, ribbon stitch with curled-up tips for others, secured in place with stab stitch. Make a one-wrap French knot in the centre. Form the longer yellow stamens in pistil stitch or use ribbon or straight stitch. Work the white spathe in ribbon in whipped back-stitch and the leaves in ribbon or detached chain-stitch. Work the smaller leaves of the large pink flowers in the same stitch. Use straight or back stitch in thread to form the stems and the veins on the leaf. Form the pink petals in ribbon stitch or ribbon stitch with curled-up tips. Use single knotted stitches made close together to form the yellow centre. Cut, trim and fluff the stitches for a furry texture.

STRAIGHT BORDER: BOWS

The template for this border is on page 125. Form the thin flower stems in stem or split back-stitch. Use ribbon stitch for the large greyish-green leaves and the same stitch for the light green leaves. Form the veins on the leaves and secure and re-shape the stitch with tiny stab stitches. Work the berries in two- or three-wrap French knots. Make a ribbon bow to fit the bow on the design. Secure the bow and tails in place with tiny stab stitches along the edge of the ribbon.

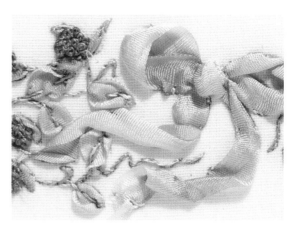

STRAIGHT BORDER: ROSE

The template for this border is on page 125. Work the thin flower stems in back, stem or split back-stitch. Working over a spare tapestry needle, make straight stitches in ribbon to form the blue petals. Use thread and tiny stab stitches to secure each stitch along the tip of the petal. Make the leaves of the blue flowers in ribbon stitch, and secure each leaf at the tip with a stab stitch. Form the leaves of the pink roses in fly stitch. Start with a straight stitch at the tip and make two or three fly stitches close together to form the shape of the leaf. Work over the pink roses, which will be added on top later. Make a two-wrap French knot to form the centre of the rose. Form the petals in ribbon stitch (see ribbon-stitch rose on page 56) and secure the tips of the petals in tiny stab stitches.

ROUND MONOGRAM BORDER

The template for this border is on page 126. Use stem or split back-stitch to form the curves of the inner circle, then all the circles in the relevant colour threads. Work from flower to flower to form the square blocks in straight stitch. Pull the thread taut as you form the next stitch so that the stitch lies snugly against the fabric. Working from the centre outwards, use ribbon stitch to form the pink petals, then the blue petals. Use tiny stab stitches to secure the petals of the pink and blue flowers. Attach a light gold bead or make a three-wrap French knot in the centre of each flower.

Working from the outer circle inwards, make a detached chain-stitch with a long anchoring stitch to form a leaf and stalk at the same time. Neaten the base of the chain with a grab stitch. Use a stab stitch or two on the end of the stalk to cover any holes in the fabric. Add a navy blue bead for the blue dots on the circle. Add golden highlights with two-wrap French knots at the base of each pink flower petal on the inner circle. Add silver highlights in straight stitch alongside the turquoise lines and back stitch alongside the green lines of the inner circle.

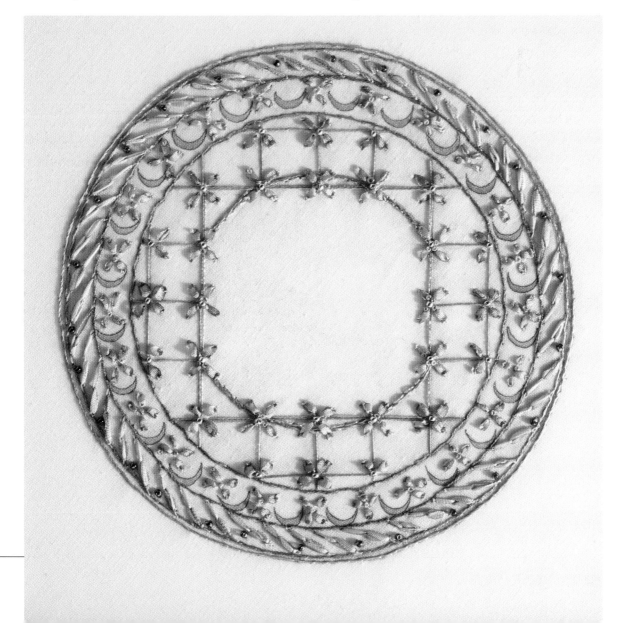

HORSE-SHOE MONOGRAM BORDER

The template for this border is on page 126. Form the green stems in stem stitch; whip some stitches to form thicker stems. Use back stitch for very fine stems, straight stitch for the leaf stalks and thorns, and two-wrap French knots for the round shapes. Form the pink stems, stalks and thorns in the same way. Use detached chain-stitch for the rose buds, twisted rib-bon- or fly- stitch to form the green part of the bud, and a grab stitch to neaten the base of the detached chain-stitch. Add the pink or gold detail at the tip of the bud in straight stitch. Use three-wrap French knots made close together to form the centre of the rose. Work the open petals at the base of the rose in ribbon stitch over a spare tapestry needle for loose, raised petals. Make a stem-stitch rose, working over a spare tapestry needle to form soft, raised petals. Push the petals upwards or downwards with your fingertips to form a realistic rose and secure the tips of the petals in place with tiny stab stitches. Add more French knots in the centre of the rose. Use detached chain-stitch for the large leaves; neaten its base with a grab stitch. Make a ribbon stitch for the smaller leaves. Use tiny stab stitches to secure the tip and base of the leaves. The tiny straight leaves leading off the stem are made in straight stitch. Whip some sections of the green stem in pink to add highlights, others in gold for gold highlights. Add straight stitches between the green leaves and on the pink buds.

'KINDNESS GROWN HERE' CARD

The template for this angel is on page 128. Start with the words, working whipped back-stitch in two strands of thread for *kindness grown here* and back stitch in one strand for *plant kindness*.

Use back stitch to outline the black lines on the apron, sleeve, bucket and shoes. Fill in the shoes with satin stitch. Make two little back stitches for the angel's eyes and use French knots to form the black body of the butterfly. Use a black bead for the head and pistil stitch for the antennae. Form the twirled path of the butterflies in running stitch.

Work the long, thin stems of the flowers with ribbon and twisted straight-stitch, the pointed leaves in straight stitch. Use detached chain-stitch for the large pointed leaves and make three or four fly stitches close together for the large, wide leaves. Work blanket stitch around the rim and base of the bucket, around the heart on the apron and the orange wings of the butterfly. Outline all the butterfly wings in back stitch. Use silk ribbon and a straight or ribbon stitch to form the larger wings. Use stab or back stitch in thread to form the veins and use French knots for the dots. Use a bead for the head, or fill it in with French knots. Form the butterfly bodies in straight stitch or French knots. Complete the antennae in stem or back stitch with a French knot at the tip, or use a pistil stitch.

Use French knots to form the dragonfly's body and head, pistil stitch for the antennae, ribbon stitch for the wings. Add the dots on the wings with French knots. Work the green lines on the apron and the angel's wings in whipped back-stitch. Outline the dress and apron in stem or back stitch and make a two-wrap French knot for the dots on the dress. Outline the *plant kindness* plaque in stem or back stitch; use whipped chain-stitch for the gold halo on the plaque. Work the stems and leaves in feather stitch, add a three-wrap French knot for the orange flowers.

Work the dark purple flowers in silk ribbon and French knots; use straight stitch for the pink and blue daisy petals. Add French knots to complete the centre of the daisies. Work the angel's dark strands of hair in straight stitch; use single-knotted stitch to form loops of hair. Cut and trim the loops for hair-like texture.

'BEE HAPPY' CARD

Embroider the words in thread using back stitch on the narrow part of the letters, and chain stitch on the wider sections. Whip the stitches with the same thread.

Outline the apron in stem stitch, its stripes in back stitch. Make a three-wrap French knot in the centre of the pink roses on the apron and complete as spiderweb roses. Work the leaves in straight or ribbon stitch. Make the black dots with three-wrap French knots, outline the pockets and hem and make the stripes in back or running stitch. Outline the beehive on the apron in stem stitch, adding golden highlights here and there in straight stitches. Make three-wrap French knots for the white dots. Outline the dress and work the stripes on the collar in back stitch.

Outline the wings in stem stitch and form the squares in straight stitch. Fill in the crown in satin stitch, forming the dots with a two-wrap French knot, and add the black outline in running stitch. Use single knotted stitch to form loops of hair. Cut the loops and trim.

Form the dark brown, yellow and golden brown stripes on the bees with closely-packed French knots (one or two wraps) or use single knotted stitches close together, cut the loops, trim them and fluff. Use stem stitch for the antennae and a one-wrap French knot for the eyes. Work the tiny bee in the right-hand corner in straight stitch and the twirled path of the bees in running stitch. Make a ribbon or straight stitch over a spare tapestry needle for the wings, with tiny stab

stitches for the veins and to secure and re-shape the wings if necessary. Form the bees on the apron with one-wrap French knots, their wings as before. The rope is worked in stem stitch with three beads attached to each end.

Form the stems of the blue flowers in twisted straight-stitch, the leaves in ribbon or straight stitch. Vary the ribbon colours for the petals, using a two-wrap French knot. Work the long stems of the roses in twisted straight-stitch, the leaves in ribbon stitch, secured with tiny stab stitches. The roses are worked in pinks, in ribbon or stem-stitch roses (see pages 56 and 57).

Outline the large beehive, form the lines in stem stitch and use straight stitch for the blades of grass between the flowers.

Templates

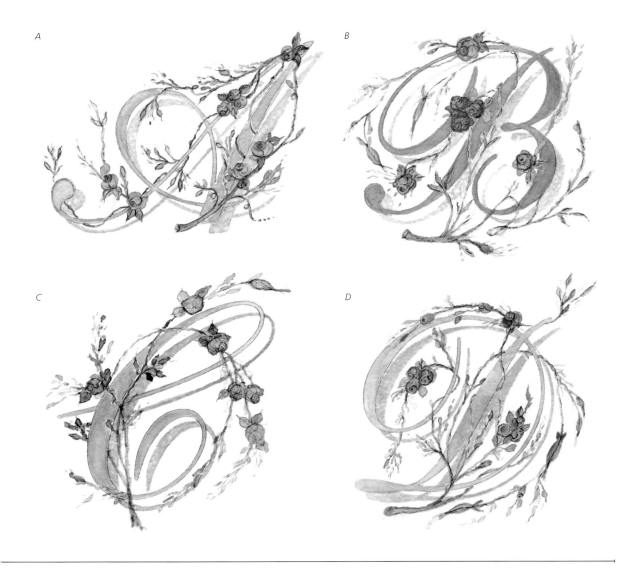

A

B

C

D

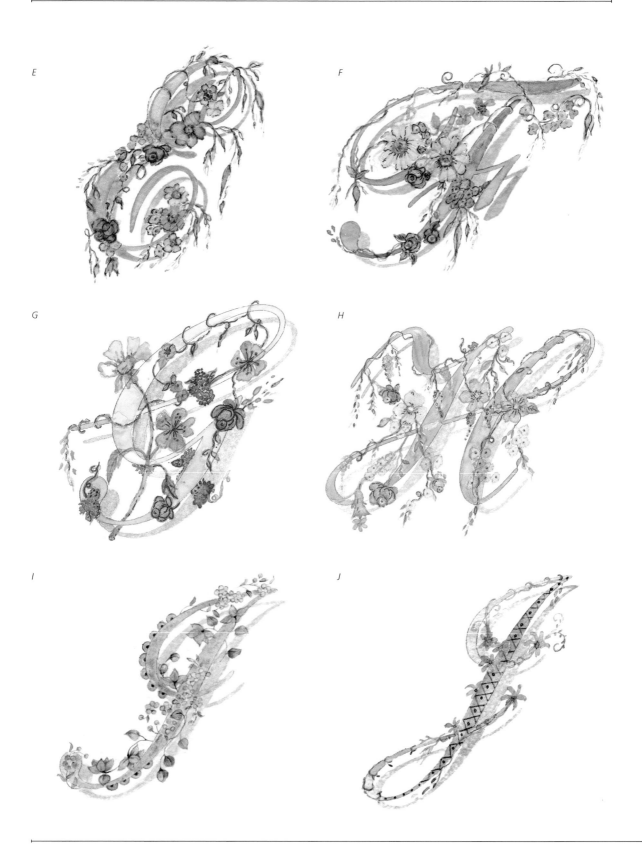

E

F

G

H

I

J

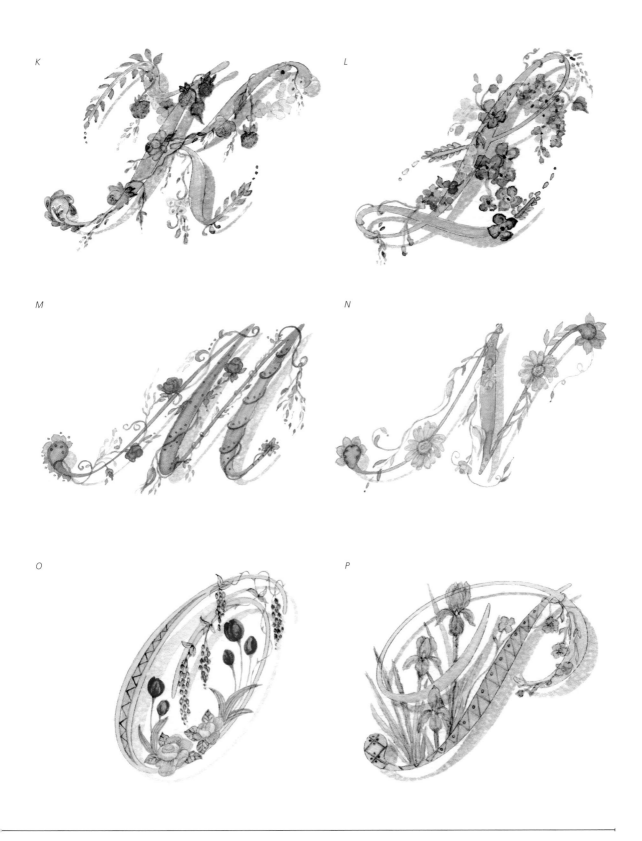

K

L

M

N

O

P

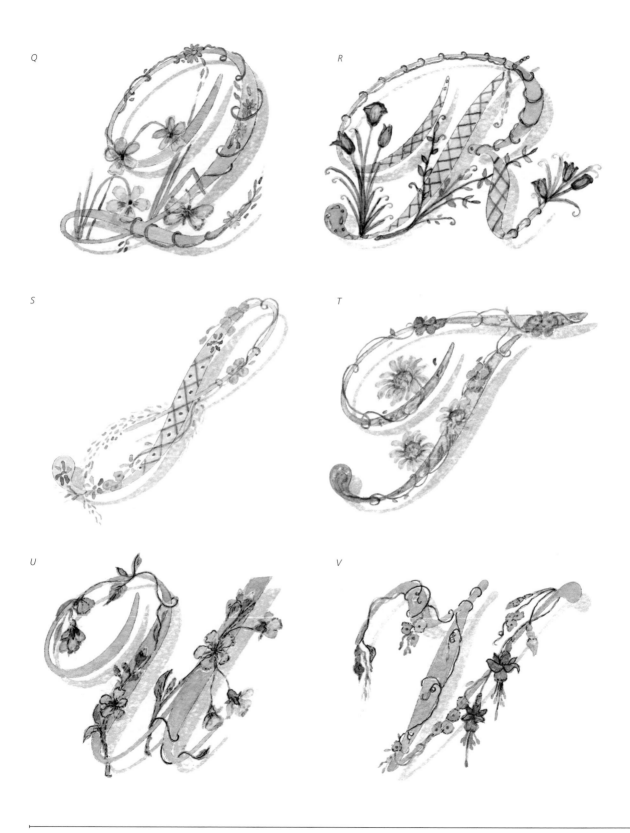

Q

R

S

T

U

V

W

X

Y

Z

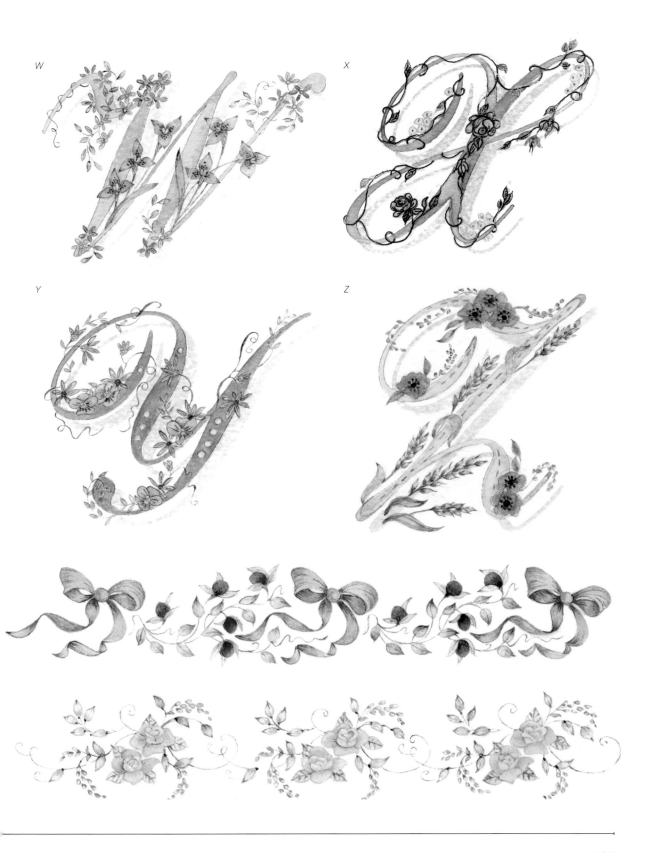

Thank You

Welcome

Happy
Happy
_Birth
Day!_

_I
love
You_

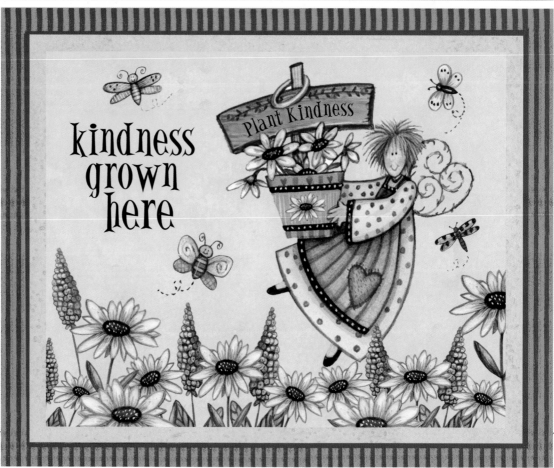